J.P. WEBSTER

VANISHING PHILADELPHIA

RUINS OF THE QUAKER CITY

Charleston   London

THE History PRESS

Published by The History Press
Charleston, SC 29403
www.historypress.net

First published 2014

Manufactured in the United States

ISBN 978.1.62619.593.6

Library of Congress CIP data applied for.

VANISHING
PHILADELPHIA

This book is dedicated to those who share my enthusiasm for Philadelphia history, photography and urban exploration. Most of all, to my loyal friends who have stuck with me through thick and thin and ventured with me into Philly's dark underbelly.
This one is for you guys.

A frozen winter night in North Philly highlights its dark buildings and rusty snowcapped exhausts—the bones of an American industrial leader. Its genius and muscle once provided some of the best products ever manufactured on planet earth and branded the phrase "Made in America" into the annals of history.

CONTENTS

ACKNOWLEDGEMENTS

I would like to thank those in my inner sanctum who assisted me in this nerve-wracking process of compiling history. First, my mother, Sue Webster, for being the best teacher anyone could ask for and for tolerating me during this stressful project. Then my father, Ed Webster (RIP), for my love of history, photography and the unknown. A big thanks goes to Dave Brown for his generosity, which proved essential in making this book. I am also very grateful for the kind assistance of the following, without whom this book would not be possible: Susan Anderson and Giema Tsakuginow at the Philadelphia Museum of Art, Cynthia Buffington at Philadelphia Rare Books and Manuscripts, Hannah Cassilly at The History Press, Clete Graham at the Wanamaker Building and Bruce Lafferty at the Athenaeum. Thanks and shouts go to Alison Bennington, Gary Heller, Bill Montgomery, Josh Morris, Luke Papa, Ed Stradling, the whole DesolateExile crew and everyone else I've hung out with in the "abandonlands."

INTRODUCTION

Philadelphia is one of America's most historic cities and has been hailed as the "Cradle of American Democracy." As the birthplace and former capital of the United States, our great history is not merely displayed in important showpieces like Independence Hall, the Liberty Bell or the Constitution Center. Nor is it exclusively linked to any one of the city's long list of American "firsts," such as the first bank of the United States, the first public hospital, the first volunteer fire department, the first public lending library or the nation's first public zoo. No, in Philadelphia, history is everywhere. From its skies to its culverted streams and from its roads to its rivers. From its buildings to its bedrock and from its charity to its crime, Philadelphia *is* history.

As the 135 square miles that make up modern Philadelphia were filling up with homes, industries and tangible ethnic barriers, the city's physical landscape was forced into a metamorphosis. A smorgasbord of row homes, factories, stores, banks, churches, firehouses, police stations, schools, hospitals, theaters, parks, cemeteries and railroads—all clustered together like a shopping mall. It was this marriage of community, industry, economy and an almost unique sense of "Americanism" that gave Philadelphia the titles of "Workshop of the World," "Athens of America" and, of course the "City of Brotherly Love." But with its delicate scales so easily upset, the bigheaded city also presented its risk-takers with an unquenchable thirst for power and domination of this majesty, resulting in Philadelphia's seasoned relationship with corruption.

It has been said that a good history, at least one with an enjoyable learnability, is a well-balanced story, comprising about equal parts joy and pathos. Since the nation's founding, Philadelphia has embraced its vital role in American history, capitalizing on it whenever possible—both for the pity of its sorrows and the attention of its accomplishments. However, more than three centuries of politics, war, technology, economic changes and forceful population shifts have created the craggy landscape that is Philadelphia today. Therefore, its habit of recording its proud historical significance has waned almost completely away. Most American cities have shifted from their manufacturing roots, having learned the lessons of their older counterparts. But Philadelphia, the nation's stubborn overachiever, never seemed quite able to forego these old-fashioned American values—industry, production, *building*. As the city's biggest strength, this proud labor-based cultural trait has seemed to hang on through the generations and, for better or worse, has shaped the modern city's collective face.

Given its proud patriotism and urban lineage, Philly is in a real kerfuffle. Philadelphians seem to have long possessed an almost vain sense of homegrown regality, stemming from the city's primal habit of thriving on its own past. But today things are very different. Like anything that decays, Philadelphia's appearance has changed slowly, not instantly. The half million row homes and mansions that used to belong to families whose names titled their streets are in various stages of decomposition. The shuttered factories that rise above that sea of squares and rectangles were once the employers of a city and the pioneers of American technology. However, three busy centuries have killed, buried, dug up and reincarnated Philadelphia many times over. And yet history has managed to hang on, in both physical and metaphysical forms. The Workshop of the World has decayed into a fascinating set of historical skeletal remains.

Nuances of Philadelphia's stubborn culture are still very much alive in the second decade of the twenty-first century. And as before, old becomes new again as sections of the city recently thought of as hopeless ghettos—such as Brewerytown and Northern Liberties—are slowly seeding toward re-gentrification. The abundance of crumbling historic structures that clutter the city were part of the reason its mid-twentieth-century inhabitants fled to the suburbs. Ironically, today it is these same fragile structures that have become coveted by a new wave of history buffs. Recently, there has been a rejuvenation of interest in what had simply been the inconspicuous past to the last of the city's pre–baby boomers. But to a curious new generation of millennials, the unsettling physical remains of this mysterious past are anything but boring.

As such, the act of exploring and photographing vacant buildings is by no means a new trend. But it would take the power of the Internet to fuel this little-known hobby into an over-the-top commercialized branding known as "Urban Exploration" or "Ruin Porn." For many, the sheer act of trespassing somewhere they don't belong is unfortunately the driving thrill. Some sadly take advantage of the dying structures by way of graffiti and vandalism. For others, the photographic opportunities are the interest. But when it comes to a fascination about American history, Philadelphia's long list of abandoned sites has proven a mecca to its committed urban explorers.

The locations in this book were not necessarily selected for their individual histories—Philadelphia includes myriad other locations with interesting pasts. They were also not chosen based on size, age or condition—the city is host to hundreds of examples of historic architecture that range from freshly vacated to crumbled ruins. The locations presented here were selected because each is an arterial vein in Philadelphia's beautiful body of history.

Without the vital existence of each of these entities, the city would not be the wonderful, enigmatic caricature of Americanism that it is today. There could be made many volumes chronicling Philadelphia's mysterious abandoned sites. This book is merely an attempt to highlight one shade of this vibrant collage of American culture from the perspective of the rotting remains of the City of Brotherly Love.

CHAPTER 1

POWER

Not long after the Civil War, in the crucible of the Industrial Revolution, new ways of creating power were in high demand. Following Thomas Edison's lead, several eager young electric companies sprang up in Philadelphia. Most of them failed or were bought out by others before the turn of the twentieth century. The Philadelphia Electric Company (PECO) was essentially a consolidation of what remained of these companies. Backed by the city's biggest banking firms, PECO eventually became a monopoly, but not without years of legal fights and personal vendettas with other utility and holding companies, such as the United Gas Improvement Company (UGI). Although at first many Philadelphians distrusted and openly feared the new technology, PECO became the longest-standing (and most profitable) utility company in Philadelphia history.

As large, influential corporations often did (and still do), PECO has had its share of scandals and power trips. Its varied leadership showed both honesty and crookedness, determination and passivity. But its presence in Philadelphia was always an overwhelming one. The company can, however, be credited with transforming the city's rambling, pre-industrial grid into the powerhouse it became in the early twentieth century. By monopolizing the electrical power industry, PECO—on its own quest for electrical domination—actually strengthened the torque of much of the city's manufacturing drivetrain in the process and revved the engines of Philly's industries for the whole world to see. Today, Philadelphia's love/hate relationship with PECO has never been stronger. Although no longer a monopoly, the company continues to serve well the industries and communities of southeastern Pennsylvania. This chapter will focus on the impact PECO had on Philadelphia, as well as the landmarks it left behind.

The undeniable presence of Philadelphia Electric Company's hulking Delaware Station is clear in this aerial photo. The coal receiving tower at the foot of its pier constantly fed the station from the daily traffic of supply barges.

Philadelphia Electric Company's Riverside Generating Stations

THE AGE OF ELECTRICITY exploded in Philadelphia at an interesting time in its history. The second and third decades of the twentieth century presented Americans with the simultaneous, polarizing forces of decadence and altruism. Prohibition divided the country and created organized crime. But at the same time, dazzling new technological wonders kept American entrepreneurialism alive. The economy was a very tall house of cards; those who lived at the top had lovely views, but they had taken real financial risks to get there. Within these two decades, Philadelphians experienced a roller coaster ride of change and turmoil. Although the Philadelphia Electric Company became a monopoly and, along with other utility companies, dominated the region politically and economically, it also created some of the most elaborate and technologically advanced generating stations then in existence on the planet.

When a passerby on Interstate 95 or a visitor to Penn Treaty Park eyes the giant "Greek temple with smokestacks" at the edge of the Delaware River in Philadelphia's Fishtown section, they often do not even realize what it is. According to one Penn Treaty Park visitor, it's "umm, a museum or something." From the ground, the massive structure easily resembles a museum or similar public building. But this museum has been closed for quite a long time. In fact, sitting just feet from the site of William Penn's famous treaty with the Leni-Lenape Indians, PECO's Delaware Generating Station *is* something of a museum—a concrete and steel memorial to ingenious engineering, to American determination in response to demand and to the Gilded Age of lawless bureaucracy.

The coal-powered generating stations built by PECO after the First World War exhibit a strong sense of permanence and industrial dominance. Their designers—John T.

Windrim and William C.L. Elgin—clearly did not foresee a time when PECO's political or financial roots would ever dry up or that a new way of producing such massive electrical current would ever be discovered. The intricate process of blending physics, mechanical and electrical science, feasibility of operation and sheer size into a method of creating and maintaining a constant flow of enough electrical current to power entire neighborhoods is difficult to comprehend by most even today. But the process of successfully designing, engineering and constructing that new science into a physical reality is almost mind-boggling.

Soon after PECO had conquered its early opponents and gained some political and financial clout, its first industrial-sized generating station was erected. Situated on the east bank of the Schuylkill River at Christian Street, the Schuylkill Generating Station (today called the Christian Street Substation) was built in 1899 to feed the western portion of center city and the growing neighborhoods of South Philadelphia. Its two turbines proved under capacity in just a few years. The future of power was clear, and it was going to be expensive. By today's standards, the ridiculous size of the structures that needed to be constructed around every major metropolitan area would be completely unfeasible. But at a time when natural gas was the preferred method of lighting, PECO's intimidating new product was a hard sell to a hard-nosed, contented Philadelphia. The daring company's bold idea was to lure the weary public in by erecting large, purposeful utilitarian buildings to display a sense of surety and permanence.

Meanwhile, the United Gas Improvement Company (UGI), which had control of nearly all of the city's natural gas supply, was growing in size as it, too, absorbed dozens of its small competitors. The outspoken founders of UGI had enjoyed an unchallenged reign over the city's heat and lighting contracts.

They were mostly members of the "City Hall Gang"—the corrupt Republican political faction that ran city government in the early twentieth century—and they definitely saw PECO as a threat to their utility monopoly. The Gang was an unstoppable political force, reaching into almost every department of city and state government. Although PECO's board of trustees also contained many of UGI's board members, PECO appeared, at least from a historical perspective, to be the underdog. The same members of Philadelphia's corrupt elite would have their turn at the helm of both monopolies, and the natural progression of the city's political system would deliver good and bad leaders to both. At its early development, UGI had the financial backing of Philadelphia business barons Peter Widener, William Elkins, Thomas Dolan and Jeremiah Sullivan; it was hard to say no to it or them.

Under its first president, Joseph B. McCall, PECO got off to a remarkable head start. McCall was a known opponent of the Gang and did battle with the old powers to earn his reputation. He was not, however, without his share of instigation or muckraking. In 1904, for example, a political hurdle came at PECO when the company reached the stage of its progression in which it needed to establish a delivery system of power lines. Prohibited by the Gang to dig its own conduit trenches and install its own lines, PECO would be forced to subcontract the work out to another Gang-controlled firm and pay almost twice as much for the work. But it was the only "legal" way.

The well-established, Gang-affiliated Keystone Telephone Company, meanwhile, owned 10 million feet of underground conduit, which carried its lines. The president of Keystone was John Mack—a tough, wealthy, Gang-loyal colleague of McCall's. McCall decided that it would be worth his while to attempt to gain friendly permission to lease or rent the use of Mack's conduit. But when McCall inquired at

Delaware Station resembles a Greek temple with smokestacks. Upon its completion, it was hailed as the largest and most technologically innovative power plant in the world. At right, its ash chutes once filled two dozen rail cars daily with the station's byproduct.

Keystone about a meeting with Mack, he was met by his "representative," none other than Philadelphia's Republican Gang leader Israel W. Durham. To McCall's advantage, an agreement was made with the "Boss of Philadelphia" wherein PECO would buy out all of Keystone's conduit for $2.5 million. McCall agreed, and the deal went through, apparently without Mack's knowledge or approval. Upon hearing of the deal, Mack claimed that he wanted $3 million for the conduit but quickly settled down after being humiliated in the courts by Durham's judicial hierarchy. It is doubtful that Mack's decision to sell off his business assets was by choice—or at least by his choice.

McCall was fire-branding his successful reputation into the ears of Philadelphia's bigwigs. Working closely with PECO's top industrial engineer, William C.L. Elgin, McCall brought the technical aspect of PECO's operations to the forefront of its advertising. Between 1900 and 1907, the company's total footage of high-tension cable tripled to 448,509, its underground conduit footage more than doubled to 6,885,847 and its customer base rose from 8,145 to 22,973. If there is one individual who can be credited with laying the framework for the rise of the Philadelphia Electric Company, it is surely Joseph B. McCall.

PECO's official architect, John Torrey Windrim, was the son of famed Philadelphia architect James Hamilton Windrim, who had held several political designations in the city. The elder Windrim was the director of the departments of water, streets, gas, lighting, surveys and public works during his long career. He was also the official architect of Stephen Girard's estate, designing several buildings at Girard College, as well as the lavish Masonic Temple at Broad and Filbert Streets. John obviously followed into his father's profession, likely inheriting many of his contracts through James's deep-rooted political clout. He designed some of the most iconic buildings in Philadelphia, as well as some of the most innovative industrial architecture in America. When James Windrim was appointed city architect in 1892, young John saw to the day-to-day operations of his father's new office. Upon James's death in 1919, John stepped up to fill his shoes. Windrim's more popular work, such as the Franklin Institute Science Museum, still dazzles younger generations of Philadelphians today.

Windrim and Elgin labored together at a hurried pace, working around politics, economics and rival electrical companies. Their creativity, it would seem, did not suffer. A new layout and technique was imagined for Schuylkill Station's new sister. It would be "the big one," a palace of power that would be sufficient to provide for one of the city's most populated areas—the textile and garment districts of Kensington and Northern Liberties. The Delaware Generating Station would introduce new mechanical and technological methods and set the standard for coal-burning power stations. It would also introduce an attractiveness and artistic merit to industrial design—with its turreted Greek Revival façade and its logo-embossed profile—creating a look not yet seen in utilitarian architecture. At the same time, the new flagship station would attempt to subliminally convey to the public a subtle notion of rock-solid integrity and modern progress, as if trying not to disturb the overly critical city.

About ten acres of land along the Delaware River, bordering Penn Treaty Park's eastern edge, was purchased from the Neafie and Levy Shipyard in 1912. Neafie and Levy had for a century been building ships at the site. Several hundred wooden ships were built there, including the cruisers *St. Louis* and *Denver* and torpedo boats *Chauncy Barry* and *Bainbridge.* The location of the old ship works provided easy access to a steady supply of coal via river barges as well as existing rail. Work on the Delaware Generating Station—named for the river that fed it—began in 1917. It was halted, however, after only a few months due to material shortages caused by the First World War. The site was closely guarded throughout 1918 due to fears of a German attack. Construction eagerly continued in 1919, hurried by the pressures of an intense postwar industrial boom.

The Stone & Webster Company—one of the world's greatest industrial construction and engineering firms—was granted the contract for construction. It began the work by excavating the ground almost twenty feet down, through layers of mica schist, to bedrock. The bedrock was found to meet the necessary support standards of a mind-bending five to six tons per square foot. To drop the caissons below the bedrock as required, two ten-ton steel driving masts (in the shape of bullets)—repeatedly hoisted above the rock on cables and dropped onto a breakpoint—were used to break through the stone. The masts were also backed by the power of a steam hammer, which struck them just after each drop. Pumps then had to be put in place to keep out the constantly flowing groundwater.

Original building plans called for the use of brick and terra cotta, but war shortages and a huge cost reduction led to the use of concrete instead—lots of concrete. In fact, upon the building's completion, after using up more than fifty-thousand cubic yards of concrete, it was hailed by Stone & Webster as the largest concrete power plant in the world. Pour-in-place concrete required the erection of wooden casing to hold it in place while it dried, and a building this big required—as estimated by Stone & Webster—1,125,000 square feet of concrete form casing. The *Stone & Webster Journal* reported that the total number of men employed in the construction of the Delaware Generating Station was

2,345. According to the same report, the construction required the use of 850 carpenters, 250 electricians, 125 pipe-fitters, 550 laborers, 170 pile-drivers, 190 steel workers and 210 miscellaneous workers.

The station consists of two original units, the older being the southern unit fronting Penn Treaty Park. It contained turbines one and two (two smokestacks per turbine) and was capable of churning out 60,000 kilowatts of electricity per hour. Both turbines were in use and under load by December 1920. Almost immediately, work began on the second unit, containing turbines three and four. By 1923, all four 35,000-kilowatt turbines were in operation, putting out 120,000 kilowatts per hour. Of course, by then even more power was needed. However, acquiring additional financial backing proved easier with its new record for success, and PECO again moved to raise the bar on the electrical industry.

Windrim, again working closely with Elgin, produced a design for

A portion of Delaware Station's large green-tiled embossment—"The Philadelphia Electric Company"—acts as an appropriate subtitle for this 2006 photo. The concrete tower at left houses the plant's central water reserve tank.

another new generating station. Following the growing residential city up the river, the site for the Richmond Generating Station—at the mouth of the Frankford Creek—was chosen to serve the growing north and northeast. Very aware of PECO's higher budget, Windrim really outdid himself. The new plant and its many clever design highlights would not disappoint. Thinking forward to solve the problem of future capacity insufficiency, Windrim and Elgin designed the building in "linked units." One unit included a set of two turbines and the appropriate supplements (the building made up two units). The units could easily be connected at the side to another set of units, and another, as the demand for power increased. An architect's rendering shows Richmond's linked unit plan—a virtual tripling of the current building, featuring two separate coal piers.

The same basic construction method used for Delaware Station was revamped for its larger sister, and Stone & Webster again undertook its construction. When placed into service on November 24, 1925, the Richmond Generating Station was already regarded as the largest and most innovative power plant in the world. Employing more than five hundred workers daily, the enormous, elegant power plant showed that Windrim and Elgin had perfected the style that had gotten its start with Delaware Station. The first two turbines were operating at a capacity of almost 200,000 kilowatts per hour. In 1926, Richmond received its third turbine, bringing the capacity to 250,000 kilowatts per hour. Meanwhile, company president Joseph B. McCall's continuing health problems caused a reduction in his duties, which had already been limited almost to supervision.

In 1924, McCall was relieved of the presidency and named chairman of the board, a position he held until his death in January 1926. Succeeding McCall as president was his close friend and business associate Walter H. Johnson. Johnson climbed into the cockpit of a very powerful machine. Thanks to the work of McCall, the position of president came with some very important political and business connections already in place. Johnson recognized that McCall had taken the company to levels once thought impossible and was due much credit. At an annual board meeting in 1926, Johnson paid tribute to his late friend and mentor:

Joseph B. McCall, from whose monument—the Philadelphia Electric Company—invisible links stretch to almost every main industry and by far the greater number of hearthstones in the city he lived, was a businessman of genius and rare discernment. He was a pioneer in the great electrical industry that is revolutionizing the world, and one of the four or five outstanding executives of light and power companies serving American centers of population.

Under the years of McCall, the company took pride in the treatment of its employees, as well as its open-door financial policy with the public. Under Johnson, the company grew even more. By his third year as president, PECO's customer base had gone up by almost 150,000 new households to 495,000. He also worked at getting the company's new headquarters built. Still standing today as part of Thomas Jefferson University Hospital, PECO's office tower at Ninth and Sansom Streets is a handsome Art Deco skyscraper. The twenty-three-story building, officially known as the Edison Building, was designed by John Windrim. Opening in 1927, it was a sign to the city and the world that the Philadelphia Electric Company was here to stay.

Also under the guidance of Johnson, PECO erected the Willow Steam Plant, which was placed into operation in 1927. Located at Ninth and Willow, the Windrim-designed plant was the company's first real effort at steam distribution. With the hired help of engineering firm Day and Zimmerman, PECO began putting in place a network of steam lines around center city. By erecting the new plant farther up Ninth Street from the new headquarters building, which also featured steam boilers in its basement, the company could connect the two buildings with a single line beneath Ninth Street. From there, lines stretched out to the east and west beneath Sansom Street and connected to buildings and other branch lines. Although ultimately not as profitable as electrical service, the production and distribution of steam did enlist several new customers, and some buildings in center city still use steam heat today.

This architectural rendering from 1925 demonstrates PECO's conceptual linked unit plan. Windrim's drawing shows Richmond Station tripled in size and capacity. The company never needed to carry out the expansion, however, as its efforts evolved into nuclear power. *Courtesy the Athenaeum of Philadelphia.*

An aerial view of Richmond Station shows its atrophied muscle mass. An intricate maze of ironwork that once collected, routed and deposited the plant's host of required ingredients into place has withered into a jungle of rust.

The mid-1920s, however, were definitely UGI's years. Upon Arthur W. Thompson's succession of Samuel Bodine as president of UGI, its comeuppance was swift and thorough, almost mechanized. In 1925, the unscrupulous, politically connected gas trust bought out one of its bigger competitors, the American Gas Company. Two years later, UGI also acquired the cunning engineering firm of Day and Zimmerman. It was clear that the simple gas company consolidation was reaching far beyond its business borders and was becoming a powerful political force. As UGI stock continued to rise, PECO's was slowly dropping. Talk began to circulate about the desire of UGI to absorb, and ultimately defeat, its archenemy.

Finally, in September 1927, in what was then the largest merger of public utility companies in the United States, a fat, swollen UGI at last sunk its teeth into its rival enterprise, and PECO became a subsidiary of UGI. Although probably a bitter feeling for PECO, Philadelphians seemed uniformly in favor of the consolidation. The *Evening Bulletin* spoke favorably of the two entities:

> *So far as public service goes, the Philadelphia community has been exceedingly fortunate in being served by two concerns like the United Gas Improvement Company and the Philadelphia Electric Company. Both have been progressive, enterprising, accommodating, and counting the good favor of their patrons as their chief asset.*

In February 1928, the transfer of PECO to UGI was complete, and Walter H. Johnson retired as president. Replacing him was longtime UGI colleague William Taylor. Along with him came Samuel T. Bodine and Arthur W. Thompson into top positions at PECO. Their top priority was to continue absorbing any and every possible nearby utility company. Just under a year later, the consolidation of already consolidated suburban companies brought PECO's area of operation to five divisions: Philadelphia, headquartered in center city; Delaware, headquartered in Chester; Main Line, headquartered in Ardmore; Schuylkill, headquartered in Norristown; and Eastern, headquartered in Jenkintown. The

renovated electric company under UGI also underwent a small name change—the Philadelphia Electric Company dropped the "the" and became simply Philadelphia Electric Company.

The years 1928 and 1929 were frantic ones at Philadelphia Electric's towering headquarters. Changes in vice-presidents, directors, board members and top engineers—combined with the looming financial crash—kept company president William Taylor on his toes. Fortunately, PECO wasn't the only party feeling the heat of the oncoming economic collapse. A few of its foes fell on their own swords in the scramble of the late '20s. The papers focused on the scandal-ridden Philadelphia Rapid Transit Company (PRT), whose notorious president, Thomas Mitten, had recently died.

When it was learned that the company almost bankrupted itself in its attempts to gain control of PECO to power its electric rail lines, it looked like PECO might face a totally unwanted legal hassle. But it was soon discovered that Mitten had amassed a suspicious personal fortune of $8 million, and the focus shifted away from PECO. When Mitten was eventually found guilty of milking PRT's funds for his own personal gain, his full estate was handed over to the PRT; as far as PECO president William Taylor was concerned, another one bit the dust. By the summer of 1929, the entire umbrella of UGI companies—especially PECO—was bracing for impact. As the crash hit, the company took the last comfort it could in the fact that it was now part of a larger economic interest and, it hoped, should therefore survive.

As fate would have it, at the onset of the Great Depression, PECO emerged much less scarred than it had feared. The simple fact that it had been taken over by UGI is probably the main reason it stayed afloat as its asset holders sunk beneath it. As the new decade began, PECO's officials warmed up to the idea of existing as a leg of UGI. But others foresaw a slow disempowering of the old PECO clique. One such man was the company's vice-president, Horace P. Liversidge, a bright young Drexel graduate who had come to the company in 1898, when we he was hired as an inspector. As vice-president, he brought a hip way of looking at the business to the boardrooms.

As early as 1926, Liversidge had hypothesized his fears about the UGI merger. The overwhelmingly machine-like impression that

would be given off by the utility giant would certainly damage its user-friendly customer interface. Within the first few years of the Depression, the down-to-earth vice-president's predictions would prove true. As the enormous utility holding company tightened its grip on its business assets, its individual qualities suffered. The ugly head of corruption soon reared in again, and UGI's relationship with PECO became less and less warm. The Pennsylvania governor's race focused on the mismanagement of the utility companies, and PECO again unwittingly received negative attention.

Progressive Republican gubernatorial candidate Gifford Pinchot promised to clean up the state's graft-filled utility companies, which he called "useless or worse."

According to Pinchot, those at the top of Pennsylvania's utility merger were the "cat's paw" of corruption in the tri-state area. He vowed to "break the stranglehold of the electric, gas, water, trolley, bus, and other monopolies on the cost of living and the government of the state." He squeezed out a narrow victory and strengthened his fight against UGI. In his inaugural address, he threw a few punches by stating, "The task today is to defeat the attack of the public utilities upon the rule of the people. We have no more compelling duty than to destroy the corruption upon which the power of the utilities depends."

History has written Pinchot as a good governor. Although his instigation of a frustrated public proved to be a real thorn in PECO's

Richmond Station's immense turbine hall still houses the four Westinghouse turbines that for more than half a century powered Philadelphia's demanding garment districts in Kensington and Frankford.

side, his conquest to outright destroy the public utility companies was a genuine threat to UGI as well. In 1932, Pinchot conducted a statewide investigation on the public utilities. He turned up nothing, however, and narrowed his focus back on their connections to Philadelphia's controlling banking firms. Many companies themselves voiced the opinion that the public utilities were in desperate need of regulation and reform, but most denied the presence of Pinchot's accused "power trust." Still, the majority of utility company owners strongly opposed the idea of public ownership through the sale of stocks. PECO apparently took it upon itself to embark on a quest to personalize its customer relations. Mostly due to the efforts of Liversidge, the new public relations policy helped PECO's reputation.

The Great Depression years in Philadelphia were not necessarily typical of most American cities. By then, the manufacturing metropolis had spawned so many new industries and introduced so many new production techniques that the deluge of the Depression was not able to engulf it all. The diversity of Philadelphia's products allowed it to avoid the debilitating blows that crippled other cities. The strange relationship between Philadelphia's corrupt powers, its monopolized utilities, its cliquish banking hierarchy and its plethora of industries concealed the city in the unique bubble of its own economic force field. The city's "bosses" saw to it that their financial interests did not suffer, inadvertently strengthening the working class of the city by instigating competition among its important manufactories. Although not totally legal, Philadelphia's way of dealing with the Great Depression is a shining example of the benefit of an economy with self-defense mechanisms, a trait America has apparently lost to history.

Thanks (in a way) to the willingness of the city's corrupt Republican machine to fight for its own greed, PECO doggy-paddled its way through the Great Depression. While certainly taking economic hits, the utility monopoly never seemed to significantly stumble. The winning team of William Taylor as the company's president and Horace P. Liversidge as its general manager would see the company through the harrowing Depression years. They knew how to deal with the public, the politicians and the poverty. John Zimmerman, president of UGI, often attempted to stick his fingers into PECO's

recipe for more control of the company's finances. Taylor and Liversidge, however, knew just how to keep him at bay.

Meanwhile, UGI—the oldest public utility company in the United States—continued to come under scrutiny by the Securities and Exchange Commission (SEC) for violations of the Holding Company Act of 1935. By 1940, the fight had become too much for Zimmerman, who resigned as president and was replaced by William Bodine. Bodine stepped in just in time to be hit by the SEC's stipulations. UGI was chopped down to less than half of what it had been. The SEC demanded that UGI's holdings be limited to a single integrated system that included Philadelphia Electric and the Delaware Power and Light Company. UGI's properties in Arizona, New Hampshire, Tennessee, Kansas and Connecticut were stripped away from its control.

In 1942, the brutish old Philadelphia gas superpower was forced to sell off $27.5 million worth of its properties and stocks. The broken, defeated company crawled away bitterly. PECO now made up 62 percent of its assets, and the proud holding company knew that it couldn't continue its relationship with its old rival now that the tables had shifted. In 1943, UGI announced its plans to sell off its remaining subsidiaries, and as the company's top officials bailed out and headed to join the ranks of PECO, it began to readapt to its role of an "ordinary" company, no longer holding political sway over an entire city.

PECO emerged from the ashes of a burning UGI and once again found itself an independent company. The excitement was but a flash, however, as the Second World War became the new focus of the nation. PECO's output was lowered and its projects put on hold until the end of 1945. Plans for a new station along the Delaware River to serve the growing communities of South Philadelphia had been in the works since the late 1930s. However, issues with construction contracts and difficulty getting the funding approved held up the green light on the project until the beginning of the Second World War. After only months, construction halted again.

Acclaimed architect Paul Philipe Cret, best known for designing the Delaware River (Ben Franklin) Bridge and for his contributions to the Benjamin Franklin Parkway, as well as

other landmarks in Philadelphia, was chosen to draw up plans for PECO's new station at the foot of Oregon Avenue. On a smaller acreage than the previous PECO riverside plants, the new Southwark Generating Station would be sandwiched between two very active piers. It would take some clever designing to compress the ingredients of a large-capacity coal-burning station into the cramped industrial district of Southwark. Cret's design was much more utilitarian than Windrim's previous plants. Yet it subtly contained modern-esque features, such as the glass bricks in its façade and circular porthole windows. His interesting design methods allowed for a full-capacity generating station on a fraction of the acreage by utilizing vertical space. The combination of the new design

and the new technologies that fed it proved Southwark a success. The station's coal delivery system was designed to use gravity to distribute incoming coal to the furnaces. This resulted in a taller, narrower building with much less conveyor belt footage.

Work on Southwark resumed in 1945, and the station was completed in 1947. But its capacity was updated again in the following decades. The postwar bliss had finally kicked in by 1950, and the future looked very bright for PECO. Its customer base was increasing by about 30,000 new customers per year and would continue to rise due to the development of new suburbs within its service area, such as Levittown. The city itself also grew after the war. The sprawling new northeast filled up with homes at a record pace.

A closer view of one of Westinghouse's enormous turbine generators at Richmond Station. Placed into service in 1931, its assembly required the labor of more than one hundred workers.

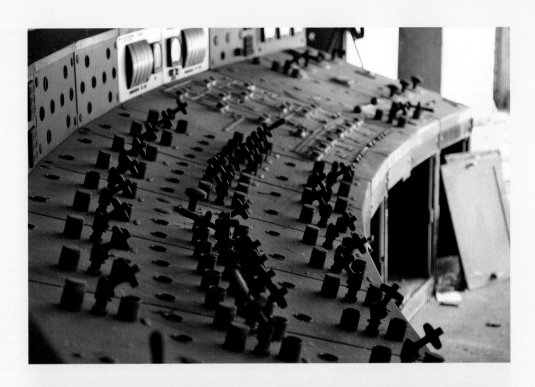

Two more turbines—powered by natural gas—were added to Delaware Station in 1954, helping greatly to carry the heavy load demanded by the city at its most flourishing period. By 1958, more than 2 million citizens lived in Philadelphia, and as new electrical appliances hit the market, the city's demand for power was never greater.

But when nuclear power was discovered in the 1960s, PECO's riverside plants began their descent out of necessity. By the 1970s, the city's grid was mostly connected to the Limerick Nuclear Power Plant, and the city's former palaces of power were slowly phased out of operation. Delaware Station's turbines were offline by 1978 and were removed from the building soon after in the first stage of its planned demolition process. But when the realization came that the gargantuan concrete structure would have to be dismantled, not demolished, the plans were put on hold, fortunately not yet seeing fruition. Richmond Station was offline by 1985 and underwent a long cleanout process. It then sat, sealed to prevent asbestos leakage, and began its relationship with rust and withering.

In 1995, Hollywood director and ex–Monty Python member Terry Gilliam, while scouting locations for his sci-fi classic 12 Monkeys, reportedly fell in love with Richmond Station upon first laying eyes on its massive turbine hall. Several scenes from the film were shot at both Richmond and Delaware Stations. According to Gilliam, it provided the exact look he wanted for the film's post-apocalyptic future setting, with "tubes everywhere, huge rusty metal tubes." Although the first, 12 Monkeys was not the last Hollywood blockbuster to integrate the unique look of Philadelphia's abandoned power plants into its storyline. In

1999, PECO embarked on the largest asbestos abatement project ever carried out in Philadelphia. The abatement of Richmond Station by the Brandenburg Industrial Service Company took—according to the company's website—seven thousand man hours. The company removed 2,552 tons of asbestos from the building's sixteen boilers and introduced new techniques to minimize employee exposure. Meanwhile, Delaware Station's natural gas turbines—the last phase of its shutdown—went offline finally in 2002.

In 2006, film director Michael Bay used Richmond and Delaware Stations rather elaborately for a sequence in his hit film *Transformers: Revenge of the Fallen*. Soon after, local filmmaker M. Night Shyamalan turned the sublevel of Richmond's turbine hall into the interior of a giant spaceship for his film *The Last Airbender*, while Delaware's turbine hall was featured prominently as a hideout for a gang of cannibals in the 2007 horror film *Tooth and Nail*. In 2009, Delaware Station's 1954 addition, housing its natural gas turbines, was demolished, revealing the original structure in its unobscured form. Both plants have been thoroughly sealed but, sadly, have experienced enough attention from scrap metal thieves to warrant the presence of a security force. Today, PECO's stations along the Delaware are coveted by their owner, Excelon Energy, which does its best to maintain them. Currently, a plan to revitalize the Delaware River waterfront threatens the plants' survival. Although efforts by local groups have raised much awareness of their importance, the future of PECO's megalithic monuments to the city's largest monopoly are uncertain.

TOP The main control board of Richmond's switch house resembles the bridge of the starship *Enterprise*. Once lit up and twinkling, this twenty-foot curved panel was the central brain of the station's operations.

BOTTOM A view from Richmond's switch house control center overlooks its engulfing turbine hall. The massive design of the plant—with its spacey, futuristic physical features—was inspiring enough to become the set of several science fiction movies.

CHAPTER 2

INDUSTRY

Once holding the title of "Workshop of the World," Philadelphia was one of America's most important industrial cities. Its wide array of factories produced everything from fabrics to fine foods. Its endless aisles of row homes were built around the sooty brick buildings that supported all facets of survival for their inhabitants. The majority of working-class families living in the city were employed by its industrial hierarchy. Old-fashioned, muscle-bound manual labor accounted for the success of this manufacturing mecca. In the daring new twentieth century, these elaborate complexes—some going back a century, using elbow grease and steam engines—were bound to clash with the age of electricity.

But even the new technological wonder of electrical power would have to fight for its supremacy in the final lap of the Industrial Revolution. New mechanical technologies would also push electrical power to its extremes, forcing it to keep up with a growing city and its constantly expanding industrial framework. As the population increased, more demand was building for goods and services; Philadelphia's industries not only stayed afloat amid traumatic financial and social changes but also pioneered new technologies and products. If Philadelphia entrepreneurs had not undertaken their fateful claims, the country as we know it today would be a noticeably different one.

Therefore, it is not surprising that buried in Philadelphia's old books and buildings and embedded into its modern physical character are many common American cultural "firsts." Taken for granted by some and completely unrealized by others, Philadelphia's historical mannerisms were the blueprint for modern American life. It seems only natural that a crowded, diverse city on the forefront of technology, spirituality, sociality and government would indeed spawn such trendsetters. The city's aforementioned manufacturing and production strength spread indiscriminately throughout its array of businesses. Interwoven closely with the city's corrupt Republican machine, these traits—and their eventual climaxes—gave birth to the Philadelphia of the twentieth century: a city that has been searching for itself ever since.

Every facet of business in Philadelphia— from investment to industry and retail to food production—possessed its own unique aspects. In some cases, such as with the Edward G. Budd Company, the product itself was the pioneering force whose mere invention and mass production changed our way of life. In other cases, as with the Freihofer and Tasty Baking Companies, a revolutionary improvement to an established work was the fortune factor. This chapter gives a glimpse into the past and present-day state of three of Philly's pioneer industrial manufactories.

Edward G. Budd Manufacturing Company

EDWARD GOWEN BUDD was born in Smyrna, Delaware, in December 1870. He studied engineering and industrial sciences in Philadelphia in the 1890s. Possessing a drive for success, Budd took his subject of study very seriously, and upon graduation, he and several other colleagues worked on steel production contracts with the Midvale Steel Company, the J.G. Brill Manufacturing Company and other local interests. Through his keen sense of innovation, Budd knew from the beginning of his career that the business of making railroad steel was probably his most profitable option. After quickly acquiring contracts, along with partners and backers, for building new all-steel railroad cars for the Pennsylvania Railroad, Budd's business really took off.

In 1912, Budd's engineering labs perfected a new method of welding pieces of steel together. The common method caused the steel to discolor and rust at the joints. Budd's method was faster, cheaper, used less material and, best yet, resisted corrosion. Fatefully, it was this technological discovery—shot welding—that set Budd's company apart from other manufacturers of shaped steel products. Buying out of his partnerships, he officially founded the Budd Company in 1912. At a small building at Aramingo and Tioga Streets in Kensington, his thirty employees began his legacy. Soon, Budd needed more space. He purchased a building not far away at I and Ontario Streets, where the company fulfilled its first contracts for the Pennsylvania Railroad. In 1913, Budd saw an opportunity in the Motor City. Upon the bankruptcy of the Grabowsky Power Wagon Company, Budd acquired its former factory in Detroit for $110,000. In it, Budd's workers produced an estimated thirty car bodies per day.

Soon the results of Budd's shot welding technique began to appeal to other branches of the growing transportation industry. He received contracts for automobile bodies by several new companies, such as Packard and Buick. As contracts continued pouring in, Budd expanded his workforce up to seven hundred full-time employees, and the thriving business soon outgrew its inhabitance. In 1914, the company moved its operations from its small Kensington site to a new building that it began leasing at the corner of Hunting Park Avenue and Stokely Street, in the city's industrial Nicetown section. Its railroad corridor offered easier access, more space and less residential surroundings.

The Midvale Steel Company's giant plant was just one block away, and other new manufactories were sprouting up in the area, such as the Tasty Baking Company down the street. By 1916, Budd's one thousand employees were producing more than five hundred car bodies per day. The company continued to make room for itself by merging with or buying out other similar companies. A new division—the Budd Wheel Company—was established in 1916 as part of the company's Detroit-based interests. Its first line of product was the steel wire wheel, of which it produced more than 250,000 in its first two years of operation. But as the year came to a close, priorities began to change.

The First World War brought Budd up from an aspiring force to a serious powerhouse. As with most industrial centers at the time, Budd was mandated by the government to shift production to supply the war effort. His plant on

Light through grimy industrial windows highlights the colors of rust and decay in this small corner of the Budd Company's gigantic 2.4-million-square-foot facility on Hunting Park Avenue.

Hunting Park Avenue began expanding to the north, south and west. The local firm of Ballinger & Perot was hired to build, and later expand, the concrete factory. In 1917, Budd received a contract from the U.S. Army Ordnance Department for 2.5 million steel helmets for America's Expeditionary Forces. The plant received shipments of square sheets of manganese steel that were sixteen square inches. Using giant presses, workers then shaped them into form. An official military corps of inspectors, stationed at the plant, was responsible for testing and approving the helmets. They had to withstand direct blasts of .45-caliber bullets and dent no deeper than a half inch. After passing inspection, they were taken to the Ford Motor Company building (later the Botany 500 company) at Broad and Lehigh Avenues, where they were painted and fitted with chin straps and lining. By the war's end, Budd had produced 1,160,829 helmets. As with many large industrial plants during the war years, Budd hired women to fill the void that the war left on his production force.

After the war, production at Budd's Nicetown plant almost doubled what it had been before the war. New contracts for automobile bodies, as well as train and even airplane bodies, were received. Expanding his facilities, Budd enlarged his Detroit plant for the manufacture of locomotive wheels. He also expanded the Nicetown plant yet again, bringing the square footage to more than 500,000. In the 1920s, Budd thrived, as his company's welding techniques and growing workforce earned it more contracts. In 1921, Budd celebrated the production of its millionth car body.

In the midst of the Roaring Twenties, Budd added more profit from contracts with auto manufacturers in France and England that paid handsomely for the use of his company's shot welding method. He also purchased the Liberty Motor Car Company of Detroit and expanded his workforce to a beastly ten thousand. The company operated six hundred presses daily until 1929, when the looming stock market crash considerably lowered auto sales. As the company's contracts began to drop away, Budd ingeniously focused efforts on research and product development. In a short time, the company created and patented another new technique: the Shotwell electric process. This allowed for the easy welding of stainless steel plates, which until then had been a difficult and frustrating task.

The Depression of the 1930s slowed Budd's momentum, but at the same time, it provided the space and opportunity for the company to get creative. It was during the first half of the decade that Budd's designers pumped out their uniquely American designs for new high-speed rail cars: Zephyrs. The Zephyr was the single product for which Budd is probably best known. Its sleek, futuristic design and stainless steel body encapsulated the Art Deco movement. The glimmering new train appeared on posters and paintings, in films and photographs, and not simply because of its totally unprecedented look—it was capable of reaching speeds previously thought impossible. At a substantially lighter weight than hulking steel trains, the Zephyr's streamlined use of stainless steel accounted for many of its key features. And thanks to Budd's new patented Shotwell process, he practically owned the future of railroad.

During the Depression, Budd also introduced the revolutionary front-wheel-drive system for automobiles, which was incorporated into new cars being made by the Citroen Company. Budd's designs for the Lincoln Zephyr and the Chrysler Airflow found their way to production in Detroit, and contracts jumped back to 1928 levels. The company actually had to hire back the thousands of workers it had laid off in 1929. By 1935, when many industries were barely staying afloat, workers at the Budd Company hardly noticed the Depression. In fact, Budd was actually opening new facilities in Europe. In

Budd's car bodies were shipped primarily via rail. In this 2012 photo, a spur of the old Reading Railroad line rounds its way into a cavernous loading bay, where product was shipped and supplies were received.

An eighth-mile-long stretch of open floor once accommodated thousands of workers every day at Budd. The plant helped build Philadelphia's economy, providing steady jobs with its private and military contracts.

1936, the company opened the Ambi-Budd Company in Berlin. It quickly became an interest of the rising National Socialist Party and was endorsed and eventually nationalized. The Ambi-Budd plant produced the Volkswagen and the Opel Kadet.

The French company Renault, after producing what it called the Juvaquatre, was sued by Budd for copyright infringement. Renault's new car was a close copy of the Kadet. Budd won the suit, further strengthening Ambi-Budd's European clout. But Budd's overseas business successes must have turned bitter rather quickly, as the inevitability of the greatest war in modern history grew nearer to America's doorstep. Budd continued good relations with his colleagues in Berlin until they became too awkward. He gradually slowed operations in Germany to a halt. The plant was soon taken over by the Nazi government.

Back at home, industries were gearing up for war. Most were transitioning production to support the war effort. Budd, however, already had everything it needed for the production of military supplies. Not only did Budd contribute to the cause, but it also became one of a small number of essential war manufacturing facilities—building tanks, treads, armored trains, jeeps, airplane bodies, specialty vehicles and equipment and weaponry. The industrial giant flexed its muscles, producing thousands of vehicle bodies in just months. As with the First World War, thousands of women were employed at the complex.

By 1942, Budd's workforce had swelled to a ridiculous twenty thousand. The demanding war brought on the need for yet another expansion. Land was purchased in Northeast Philadelphia, where plenty of room could be afforded for a new "bombproof" facility for the production of rail cars. Located on Red Lion Road near Verree Road, the new plant was operational by 1945, although its immediate schedule was ammunition production until 1946. It did not appear, however, that rebounding from war production was a difficult process for Budd. While many industries were catching their breath, Budd's facilities shifted smoothly back to full-schedule civilian production in only months.

After the fog of war cleared, Budd consolidated some of its subsidiaries, such as Budd Wheel in Detroit. It also changed its official name from the Edward G. Budd Company to the Budd Manufacturing Company. During this litigation process in 1946, the company's founder, Edward G. Budd, died in his seventy-fifth year of age. The company was carried on without losing pace by his son, Edward G. Budd Jr. In 1949, Edward Jr. spent almost $10 million expanding the powerful Nicetown operation. A new stamping plant was built in Indiana, and the Red Lion facility was further enlarged with a foundry for the production of brake drums. But before Budd's wartime production lines had time to cool down, the Korean War started them back up. Although Budd's workforce dropped by about 15 percent due to the war, its major production operations did not seem to suffer.

The Korean War actually strengthened the company further, making necessary its role as a full-time military contractor. At the Nicetown plant, a new facility was added along the western end of the property for the shaping of tank hulls, jet turbine blades, propellers and other official equipment. While seeming to constantly grow, Budd kept its progression at an even pace by breaking the giant company down into seven divisions, each dealing with a different type of production. It also consolidated its many subcontractors that built specific machinery and tools for the company. The 1950s were anything but slow. Production moved into new technologies, keeping Budd not merely in the loop but rather, in many ways, on top of it.

By 1960, almost half of Budd's production had become military-based, but at the same time, it was developing new methods in every stage of its automotive and rail car divisions. The epitome of a successful company, while creating new radar detectors in one division, Budd was simultaneously engineering and perfecting the first automotive disc brake in 1965. In 1967, Edward G. Budd Jr. retired as the company president. While still growing by purchasing other companies, such as the Milford Fabricating Company of Detroit and the Gindy Manufacturing Company of Pennsylvania, Budd was shedding the majority of its loose manufacturing skin. In 1971, Edward G. Budd Jr. died, and the company's glory days were beginning to see their end.

The 1970s were a gradual downward slope for Budd, and by 1980, its former business indestructibility had withered. By 1990, its hulking workforce numbered fewer than

ten thousand. As the company's pioneering technologies and techniques became common in the late twentieth century, the Budd Manufacturing Company took its seat among the great American industrial giants. Today, the company still exists, though at a fraction of its former size. By 2002, the company had completely relocated its operations to Detroit. When the Nicetown plant finally closed its doors for good in 2010, some interesting ideas for its reuse were tossed around.

A casino developer decided against using the property in favor of a site along the Delaware River. Hollywood actor and hometown hero Will Smith was supposedly interested in turning the property into a full-fledged film production studio to rival those on the West Coast. This plan, too, fell by the wayside. Today, Budd's dark facility looms large along a stretch of Hunting Park Avenue. Its machinery since relocated and its workforce no longer bustling, the giant concrete monstrosity has been the scene of at least one homicide since 2012. Its location, in the once thriving neighborhood of Nicetown, is the biggest depreciator of its value. Nevertheless, Budd, the chest-beating hulk of industrial power, is a name that Philadelphians will not soon forget.

ABOVE A single ray of light sneaks into Budd's enormous main floor. Although larger than many industrial plants in itself, this fifty-acre room is but a fraction of Budd's gargantuan Nicetown facility.

OPPOSITE The top floor of Budd's assembly building shows off its solid ironwork, a type of construction rarely seen today. Driven by fears of foreign attacks, accidental explosions and fires, the reinforced concrete plant was built to last for centuries.

Once the largest single bakery in the world, the former Freihofer Baking Company at the intersection of Twentieth and Indiana sits patiently, waiting for its next tenant.

Freihofer Baking Company

PHILADELPHIA'S NICETOWN/TIOGA
section was always a place full of industry. The neighborhood's factories led the way in its development, and most of their employees lived within walking distance. Today, the area is one of the city's most dangerous, and these once bustling factories today sit crumbling, lending visually to the area's rough reputation. Barely distinguishable from its abandoned industrial neighbors, the Freihofer Baking Company's large food factory at Twentieth and Indiana Streets hides its significant past from the crime and poverty surrounding it.

The disorganized structure is a collection of additions and expansions, as most of the original buildings have been replaced, demolished or hidden completely by new construction. But behind the random brick walls, the concrete additions, the natural growth and the graffiti, there remains a nostalgia—a portal into a time when Philadelphia's wide variety of neighborhoods was its very identity. A time when hot baked goods were delivered personally by the baker aboard his horse-drawn bread truck. Using the present-day neighborhood as a point of reference, it is actually difficult to picture the Freihofer Baking Company in its heyday, surrounded by acres of wheat fields and horse stables.

The Freihofer family—often locally pronounced "fry-huffer"—emigrated from Germany to Philadelphia after the Civil War. The family soon spread across the river to Camden. In 1884, Charles Freihofer opened a small bakery there. Apparently possessing a natural ability in the baking trade, Charles's bakery met with success. But it would be the intuition of his brother, William, that would set the family bakery on the road to industrial significance. When William was thirteen, he established a local milk route, for which he created a speedy delivery system. William joined the family business in 1890 and became immediately interested in the prospect of establishing a system of fast delivery of the store's baked goods throughout the urban center around Camden and, if possible, Philadelphia. By 1893, the Freihofer brothers' clever combination of baking and delivery techniques was proving very profitable. With big plans, they officially started the Freihofer Vienna Baking Company.

The brothers purchased four acres at Twenty-fourth and Master Streets in the Sharswood neighborhood of North Philadelphia and opened a larger bakery there. But by 1901, the business was already outgrowing this new facility. Following the city's northward industrial migration, the brothers purchased twelve undeveloped acres in the neighborhood of Nicetown, about one mile north. They hired the architectural and engineering firm of William Steele & Sons to design and build a new factory among open fields along the Reading Railroad's line, near the current intersection of Twentieth and Indiana. Since the area surrounding the factory was just beginning its development, plenty of room was afforded for harvest space and building expansion.

The brothers' exciting new business ideas relied heavily on their horse-and-wagon delivery system. The company's clever use of hot metal in its delivery wagons ensured that the product arrived hot and fresh. At a time when most in the city walked to their local bakery for hot bread, Freihofer's delivery system was very well received. All a customer had to do was hang the company's alert flag (which they received upon their first delivery) on their front door or window, signaling their interest in continuing delivery service. In a few short years, the brothers acquired more surrounding property, expanding their wheat fields and stables west to Twenty-first Street and north to Clearfield.

An early twentieth-century review of Freihofer's—as the bakery came to be known—from *Pennsylvania and Its Public Men* praises the company's intuition in its own turn-of-the-century way:

> In olden times when one's mother used to stand at the table mixing dough for the family consumption, it was no common occurrence for her to become fretful, annoyed and peevish. In later days these obstacles were overcome by machinery, which has done the work without any complaint from the operator, and perhaps the Freihofer Company, of Philadelphia, was one of the first to solve the perplexing problem. It almost appears astonishing, but nonetheless it is true, that they established this gigantic business in 1893 upon a small scale, and through their own individual ability and efforts they have reached such a stage

> to-day that they manufacture upward of 100,000 loaves of bread a day, giving employment to between five and six hundred hands.

In 1909, Charles Freihofer boasted to the press that he was in the process of expanding the Nicetown property into the "largest bakery in the world." He wasn't kidding. The Freihofers spent almost $200,000 turning their small business into a colossal, mechanized food production facility with its own electrical generating plant. The new sanitary ovens and roller beds, as well as the brand-new industrial-sized electric dough mixers, required a heavy load of electricity to operate. The plant received its supply of coal from the Reading's line. The enlargement of the facility necessitated the final and biggest expansion of Freihofer's delivery system. With the property now extended to contain more than two square blocks, the brothers erected what was reported at the time to be the world's single largest horse stable building, with a capacity for more than 350 horses and 160 wagons. Also contained under the same roof were wagon repair and horseshoeing shops.

The first few years of business at the giant bakery must have lived up to the brothers' hopes, as the Freihofers branched out to several other areas while still maintaining the Master Street facility and several others in New Jersey. In 1913, William Freihofer acquired property in Troy, New York, and opened another large baking plant there. By 1914, the company was employing almost one thousand workers at its two locations. In 1920, a third location was added at Fifty-second and Florence Streets in West Philadelphia. The business then spread down to Chester and Wilmington. Thanks to almost intrusive solicitation by William Freihofer himself, the company gained contracts to supply all the best restaurants in town with their bread, including the new ones in the busy lobby of the Reading Railroad Terminal.

While Charles was busy on the baking side of the business, William was using his financial expertise to expand the company's interests. William became involved with several other businesses, however, and fears surfaced about his loyalty to the family business. But he continued to faithfully run the company while also serving as president of the Northwestern

Trust Company at Ridge and Columbia Avenues. In 1916, William's son, Stanley Freihofer, also joined the company. Stanley quickly began assuming more managerial positions and carrying some of the heavier weight. The brothers soon had the Philadelphia market in their pockets, turning out their highest profits yet. As with most elite Gilded Age businessmen, the Freihofers' clout allowed for their inclusion in city affairs—political and otherwise—and made them a household name in Philadelphia culture.

When the First World War revved Philadelphia's factories to full throttle, the Freihofers did their part. Proudly offering its "Liberty Loaf," the company proclaimed that it was the only bread endorsed by the War Department and was made according to wartime shortage standards. It was generally thought that cutting back on ingredients like butter would make for a very unappetizing dough. Freihofer's, however, pulled off an impressive stunt by cleverly relabeling certain ingredients to fit in with government requirements while still containing enough dairy to hold to standard taste. The company embarked on a massive ad campaign in local newspapers and magazines, making

A cold February day in North Philly. In this view, a doorway at Freihofer's frames the face of a conflicted city, stuck somewhere between the nostalgia of its past and the promise of its future.

the most out of its voluntary but painful agreement with the War Department. It was not shy in telling customers to "save a slice of bread a day" by buying its Liberty Loaf.

At the time, bread usually went stale by the end of each day. Although this must have been very profitable for the baker, it naturally became an annoyance to the customer. Freihofer's was one of the first companies to use malt extract in its dough, thus allowing it to keep fresh for days. Its full-page ad, which peddled "large double loaves" for ten cents each, explained:

> Philadelphia and suburbs have
> over 400,000 families. If each
> family wasted one slice of bread
> per day, due to being dry or
> stale, it would mean an actual
> loss of over 30,000 loaves
> of bread daily, representing
> approximately 16,000 bushels of
> wheat each month of 30 days; or
> the appalling yearly bread waste
> in money value of over eight
> hundred thousand dollars.

William Freihofer's success and wide esteem was apparently not enough to numb the pain caused by the loss of his oldest son, Charles, who was killed in the First World War. William, in his fifties, gradually sank away from the company and finally died in 1932, leaving behind a baking legacy. Lesser known is that William—a thirty-second-degree Mason—had a strong personal interest in the movies. He funded the construction of several theaters in the first two decades of the twentieth century, including the still functioning Tower Theater. His son William Jr. continued as president of the company, bracing it for the impact of the Great Depression. Its decade-old plant in Erie, Pennsylvania, was the first casualty of the crippling financial draught, merging with the Firch Baking Company of Erie in 1933. But the Freihofer umbrella still operated thirteen baking facilities

in Pennsylvania, New Jersey and Delaware and employed more than two thousand workers. One year later, William Jr. ran unsuccessfully for Congress as a candidate from Delaware County.

When William Jr. died in 1939, his will stated that he wished the company to remain under family ownership for "as long as possible." His brother Stanley, after some convincing, agreed to run the company. However, he, too, passed away just over a year later in 1941 at age forty-seven. Fortunately for William Jr., the business stayed family-owned for another decade, as the next generation of Freihofers filled the presidency. Even after being absorbed by two other large conglomerates, members of the Freihofer family sequentially acted as the company's general manager. But as the physical neighborhood surrounding Freihofer's plant at Twentieth and Indiana began to change, and the city's industries settled into their economic niches, the company began to cut back its operations in Philadelphia. Its other facilities in New York, New Jersey and Delaware were outproducing the Nicetown plant by the close of the Second World War. Freihofer's would slowly transfer and consolidate its production facilities and business headquarters to the Troy plant, which is still operating today.

In 1949, the company sponsored a short-lived children's broadcast called *Breadtime Stories*, which shamelessly featured a cartoon rabbit named Freddie Freihofer. By 1956, Freihofer's baking complex at Twentieth and Indiana, once the largest bakery in the world, was considered primitive. Without the option of expansion in the crowded industrial neighborhood, the almost fifty-year-old bakery finally closed its doors. The building was sold two years later, and the company's operations in the City of Brotherly Love were never the same. By the 1960s, the neighborhood was experiencing its final round of "white flight," as the last of its old inhabitants

Despite the sign, this door at Freihofer's remains ajar. After a multitude of uses, the one-hundred-year-old building retains very few of its original features.

LEFT Unused for decades, a historic atmosphere lingers at Freihofer's. This ultra-utilitarian restroom is a great example of early twentieth-century industrial construction.

OPPOSITE This electric panel once fed the dozens of dough mixers at Freihofer's, as noted by the decorative, hand-painted label on the inside of the door.

relocated to the suburbs or the northeast. Property values were steadily declining, as crime and poverty continued to box-in the old baking factory. It's next occupant, a local textile company, was settled in by 1959, and the building was converted for use appropriately.

Rows of sewing tables, operated by hundreds of local employees, kept the building in full use until the 1970s, when it changed hands again. By the 1990s, the building was serving as a warehouse for arcade machines, for rent and sale to vendors. By the turn of the twenty-first century, it was a warehouse for just about anything a customer was willing to pay to store.

A local supermarket chain, Kelly's Korner, rented the newest and largest addition to the building, serving as its last tenant. It had become completely abandoned by 2003. In 2008, the dilapidated building was used to nice effect in the film *Law Abiding Citizen*, serving as the location for a grisly murder scene. Ironically, one of the country's first motion picture studios was once located just across the street from Freihofer Baking Company. Lubinville, the square-block studio complex built in 1910 by early filmmaker Sigmund Lubin, tragically burned to the ground four productive years later. Most of his flammable film stock was lost in the fire.

Today, the Freihofer Company is owned and operated by the Grupo Bimbo Company, the world's largest bread chain, and still produces its baked goods at its Troy plant. Since the Troy branch began as one of William's subsidiaries in 1913, it independently celebrated its 100th anniversary in 2013. The company's true stomping grounds, however, known today as Allegheny West, have long gone stale. Nicetown has at present one of the city's highest homicide rates but actually has improved since the 1990s. Nonetheless, the community's days of localized industrial self-support—not to mention bakeries—are definitely over. And still, many Philadelphians will never forget the classic red logo and the fresh smell of Freihofer's bread.

The main storeroom at Freihofer's (shown here in 2011) served as the shooting location for a grisly murder scene in the 2009 film *Law Abiding Citizen*.

Tasty Baking Company

AT THE BEGINNING of the twentieth century, the local bakery was far different than it is today. Bakeries and neighborhood grocery stores dotted Philadelphia's landscape by the hundreds. Through their personal connections to their communities, these local family-owned businesses once thrived and were often the places of gossip and social interaction for neighborhood residents. Usually the work of preparing, baking, wrapping and displaying the food in these local shops was performed by a single individual, commonly the shop owner. Before a solid method of food sanitation was put into place, health conditions in these small food stores were mediocre at best.

In 1913, a young man named Philip J. Baur, while working in his father's busy Pittsburg bakery, Baur Bros., became frustrated with its laborious methods of preparing food. Baur sought new ways of improving his father's business, including clever new recipes. In a year, the eager entrepreneur had impressed just about everyone he knew with his new pastries. In 1914, under the encouragement of his friends and family and armed with his arsenal of new ideas, the ambitious Baur started his own bakery. Taking the business to Pennsylvania's largest city, Baur's Philadelphia-based bakery got off to a fairly normal start among hundreds of others offering fair competition. It was not until Baur met Cleveland baker Herbert C. Morris that his new ideas began to take shape. Morris was reportedly enraptured by Baur's new recipes and production ideas, and together the two created what they called a revolutionary step in sanitation. By baking several small prewrapped cakes on a baking slab

instead of one traditional cake, the baker would never have to handle the cake post-bake. This would save time, Baur thought, and would improve the unsanitary condition of the method at the time.

As Baur and Morris were finalizing their new business venture, Morris became ill with appendicitis. While confined to a convalescent home, Morris created the title for their new product: Tastykake. With its simple, clever name, the Tasty Baking Company was officially formed in 1914. Baur's individually wrapped cakes were appealing enough to investors—thanks in large part to Morris's business connections—and the partners raised $50,000. They purchased an old foundry building at Twenty-fourth and Sedgely Streets and converted it into the first bakery of the Tasty Baking Company. After only weeks of operation, the giant ovens of the new bakery were churning out Baur's innovative product. Packaged in a small blue box displaying the slogan "The Cake that Made Mother Stop Baking" and priced at ten cents, the new treat came in three varieties—iced yellow, white and chocolate and raisin and molasses.

In October 1914, Morris—mostly recovered from his appendicitis—began peddling the pastry to neighborhood grocers in North Philadelphia, then South and then West. Local stores could not keep them on their shelves, and a demand quickly grew for Baur and Morris's trademarked cakes. By the end of the busy year of 1914, the company had grossed more than $300,000 in sales. Morris sought out more delivery routes beyond the city limits, solidifying their customer base. Sales soon extended to Baltimore via

This 2010 aerial view of the Tasty Baking Company shows its neighborhood presence, positioned along the railroad.

steamship, and dozens of new local routes were added. By 1917, yearly gross sales had risen to more than $900,000.

With the onset of World War I came the first real test for the Tasty Baking Company. The shortage of labor, combined with the scarcity of sugar, made it difficult for Baur to maintain his quality standard of superior ingredients. He spread his nerves thin trying to come up with another innovation to keep his products from becoming a casualty of the war. But while other bakeries produced stale bread from lackluster ingredients due to war shortages, the Tastykake gained even more fame as the cake that never went stale. Thanks to its original design concept, the prepackaged and sealed cakes stayed fresh. This further graced the company's roaring sales record, which by the end of the war had reached more than $2 million annually. Its customer base was spread throughout the tri-state area using trucks, trains and barges. Baur's original bout of genius turned out to be a bigger deal than he realized, and he regained focus after the war. But Baur's erratic reputation as a perfectionist who suffered from stress was proving itself true.

By 1920, the business had outgrown the old building on Sedgley Avenue, and a new food factory was constructed only a few blocks away. The new six-story building on Hunting Park Avenue near Twenty-eighth Street opened in 1922. Its location in Nicetown was just two blocks from the Edward G. Budd Company and provided seventy-two thousand square feet of space. Tasty's new production levels only increased demand throughout the Roaring Twenties. Expansion of the building continued all the way through the decade with five additions, bringing the total building area to 350,000 square feet by 1930. The first year of the Depression saw a huge drop in Tasty's sales, but Baur continued to innovate by releasing the milk chocolate–covered cake. The cakes came three to a package and were economically priced at five cents. It seemed that Baur's best work—like many innovators'—came at times of enormous national trauma.

Another of Baur's pivotal hardship-inspired ideas was the Tastykake pie in 1931, which would become the company's best seller. Through advertising in newspaper and radio, Tasty's pie was an instant success. One year later, the square-shaped pies became their current rectangular shape. The "Tastypie" was the first of its kind ever marketed in the United States and revolutionized the snack cake. New technologies allowed Tasty's officials to concentrate on developing a system of mechanized automation to produce their cakes. Their work came to a halt, however, with the outbreak of World War II. Following the war, though, sales continued to skyrocket, with gross profits reaching $16 million by 1951. Philip Baur died later that year at the age of sixty-six. His son-in-law, Paul Kaiser—a skilled insurance executive—was called on to assume the presidency of the company, which he did in 1953. Baur's partner, Herbert Morris, remained chairman of the board until his death in 1960.

The '50s were a great period for Tastykake. The company perfected its image as the maker of Philadelphia's signature pastry. Philip Baur Jr. came aboard in 1952 and was a voice for major modernization and structural changes to the company. An $8 million capital investment saw the plant revamped and restocked. New machinery and technologies filled the enlarged building's floors. When Tasty enlisted the help of engineer Alfred Gramp to develop a wax paper cake wrapping machine in 1957, its move toward mechanization—and away from manual production—marked the end of Tasty's days as a neighborhood-friendly, employee-driven local bakery and the beginning of its modern existence as a corporation. As wages slowly rose

Cargo elevators that once busily shuffled through Tasty's six sprawling floors sit silent in this 2012 photo.

ABOVE The sun finds its way into an office area at the Tasty Baking Company, where staff memos addressing its closure still hang in place.

OPPOSITE A giant pedestal on the roof of Tasty's food factory on Hunting Park Avenue once supported the building's colorful water reserve tank—a landmark visible for blocks in the 1940s and '50s.

and labor unions became more powerful, Tasty began shedding its massive workforce in favor of technology. The company appealed to customers by noting that because of technology, their hands would be the first to ever touch the cake. The automatic wrapping system was hailed as a "major breakthrough" by Tasty's president, Paul Kaiser.

In 1957, the plant on Hunting Park Avenue was enlarged for the sixth time with a 55,000-square-foot addition, housing the new mechanical and research and development departments. The continued modernization of the facility was lead by engineering director John F. Wettig and chemical engineer John N. Wurst. Antiquated ovens were replaced with large, high-speed electric models, one of which was 160 feet long. An improved delivery system

was also implemented, and it greatly cut down the amount of manpower required. Wurst described the company's progression: "Mr. Baur developed a long life for our product years ago. Our contribution has been in terms of maintaining it, while improving efficiencies and economies under the stress of increased and faster production."

In 1961, shares of Tasty's stock were opened to the market, and the company began proudly advertising its status as "publicly owned." Philadelphia's cliquish inner circle of wealth saw to it that the company, as one of its own, would be well placed in the market—and well watched. Tasty's board of directors became filled with prominent Philadelphia businessmen such as Edward G. Budd Jr., Casimir A. Sienkiewicz (CEO of the Central Penn National Bank) and Andrew B.

Young of the law firm Stradley, Ronon, Stevens and Young. By Tasty's fiftieth anniversary in 1964, the company's public relations had much improved, and it branched out its service further. The 1970s saw the rise of snack foods and convenience store candy, and Tasty's snack cakes held their own against a new wave of prepackaged junk food.

By the 1980s, Tastykake was a household name in Philadelphia and surrounding communities. Although it had a decade of good hometown recognition, Tasty's sales were beginning to feel the squeeze. The 1990s were a bit better, eventually seeing Tasty return to a slight boost in sales. A strong refocus on the company's advertising campaign showed as the new millennium began. By 2005, the company had finally dealt with its long-closeted need for a newer plant. The ninety-year-old building on Hunting Park Avenue was now in one of Philadelphia's most dangerous neighborhoods, and its facilities were becoming slowly less desirable. The company began searching for a site for a new plant, but legalities with the city drew the process out for several years.

Eventually, the Tastykake Company purchased a portion of land along the Schuylkill River just above its mouth at the Delaware and erected its new facility in 2009. The site was formerly occupied by the Tidewater Grain Company and the naval yard's brig facility. The company also built a new headquarters building in the heart of the navy yard in 2011, lending its face to the blossoming business park. The administration had completely transferred its operations from the Nicetown plant to the new buildings by the end of the year. Almost instantly, the stoic concrete building on Hunting Park Avenue fell into the hands of scrappers, squatters and graffiti writers.

Today, the Tastykake Company is one of Philadelphia's more successful businesses, employing hundreds of Philadelphians. At the time of this writing, Tasty's old food factory sits silently, awaiting restoration or demolition. While the future of the company is bright, its past is also worth remembering. How intuition and hard work raised a small business into a trendsetter is not a unique lesson in America, but the Tasty Baking Company is a unique building block of Philadelphia. In 2014, Tasty celebrated its 100th birthday by releasing some of its bestselling flavors in special packaging. Its name is one of much reverence in Philadelphia, and its slogan is as true today as it was fifty years ago: "Nobody bakes a cake as tasty as a Tastykake."

CHAPTER 3

EDUCATION

Higher education has been a showpiece of Philadelphia culture since before the founding of the University of Pennsylvania in 1756. The Philadelphia Board of Public Education was established in 1818. Its first president, Roberts Vaux, served until 1831. The small tax base of the city provided for meager but efficient school building, as well as very basic education. However, Philadelphia's method of providing free schoolbooks to its students, which began in 1819, had become the standard for American public schools by the turn of the twentieth century. As the city's population grew, its public school districts began multiplying. They appeared in random, dotted patterns throughout the incomplete city, where neighborhoods were already developed or were developing.

A new act in the state legislature finally put a solid public school system in place by 1836. The first public high school in the country—the Central High School—opened in 1838 on the current site of the Widener Building at South Penn Square. The school still exists today, four buildings and three locations later. By 1850, a board of trustees of the public schools, whose appointment was decided by Common Court judges, had proved small but effective. The board afforded for almost three dozen new schools to be erected about the city. Quaker influence was not gone from the city, and the new school system showed its charitable roots. Fortunately, graft and corruption would not work its way into the city's school system for another half century.

Philadelphia had one of the country's first municipal systems of public education, along with cutting-edge school facilities in which to employ it. These achievements, however, did not come freely to the city. Its endless line of political saboteurs and elected crooks were also part of the reason Philadelphia was financially and legally able to build such a system. Therefore, as the city grew and expanded, this system also matured and reached deeper into its municipal veins. By 1880, Philadelphia's separate school districts were numbering almost thirty. This homegrown system of tiny districts (some only a few square blocks), each containing simple, small schoolhouses that served only a few dozen students each, surely provided a sense of communal aesthetic that has long since disappeared. Schools built during the flamboyant 1870s and 1880s are almost extinct in Philadelphia. A few managed to survive, such as the rustic Cumberland School (later renamed the David Farragut Public School) at Hancock and Cumberland Streets in Kensington.

Over the years, a succession of school board architects gradually transformed the prototypical "Philly school" design that we know today, and throughout the city, schools became sequentially more uniform. In the 1870s, the official Board of Property Architects—which designed and built all public schools and buildings relating to the school board—was composed of Louis Elsler and Joseph Anschutz, along with their team of assistants. Elsler designed quaint, three- or four-room schoolhouses, most of which contained one outhouse and were heated by coal in the winter. Anschutz's designs, however, were far more ornate and usually located in wealthier areas. He designed more than seventy schools in Philadelphia, a precious few of which remain. Anschutz's successor, Henry DeCourcey Richards went a step further with the use of central boiler rooms, roof recreation areas and new fireproof construction methods. By 1911, the new public school building codes required that "all school buildings two or more stories high hereafter erected or leased in any school district of the first class in this Commonwealth shall be of fire-proof construction."

Richards's time as architect of public schools stretched into the second decade of the twentieth century, and his work still remains in no shortage throughout the city. By the 1920s, the school district's budget was at a crest, and the frequency of school construction peaked. Taking over as architect after Richards was Irwin Thornton Catharine. Catharine designed more schools in the city than any other architect, and his work includes the Board of Education Building on the Ben Franklin Parkway. Roughly 60 percent of his school buildings remain in use

today. The numerous small districts that made up Philadelphia's public school system were slowly consolidated in the decades after the Second World War. Small schools were replaced with larger, modern replacements, and the curriculum changed drastically.

Today, Philadelphia's public school system is in a sad state of operation. Its budget is lower than that of most American cities, and its graduation rates have sharply declined. Life for teachers and educators has suffered as well. Their salaries have dropped, while working hours have increased, and the teacher/student ratio has become more unbalanced than ever before. Sadly, vacant schools in the city today are plentiful, and each has its own interesting history. However, this chapter will narrow in on just one shining example of Philadelphia's disintegrating pastime of excelsior education. Hopefully, this pioneer of the American school system can regain its standing, and Philadelphia can once again take pride in the quality of its educational facilities.

Northeast Manual Training School/ Thomas A. Edison High School

This aerial view of the old Northeast High School at Eighth and Lehigh shows its deteriorated state in 2010. Visible just above the school is the long-defunct Fairhill Reservoir and its ornate pumping station.

AFTER THE CIVIL WAR, a new concept in public education took form—the manual training school. A concept inspired by the Industrial Revolution, the manual training school would teach skills in science and technology to boys. As one of many new philosophies emerging out of the flurry of emotions that followed the country's bloodiest conflict, the idea of manual training was born out of war-weary America's longing to advance as a nation. In

1926, author Paul Monroe, in his publication *Cyclopedia of Education*, wrote, "Manual training came into being partly as the expression of a new educational philosophy and partly from dissatisfaction on the part of the public with the results of the purely bookish curriculum of the schools."

The manual training schools were established in Philadelphia in 1885, taking the lead from St. Louis. Their basic course of study was as follows:

FIRST YEAR

Arithmetic (reviewed); Algebra (begun)
English Language—structure and use; study of
*   selected classics*
United States History and Civil Government
Physiology and Physical Geography
Freehand and Mechanical Drawing
Shop Work—carpentry and joinery, wood
*   carving, wood turning, pattern making;*
*   Proper care and use of tools*

SECOND YEAR

Algebra (finished); Geometry (begun)
Physics—experimental work in the physical
*   laboratory; Principals of mechanics*
English Composition and Literature—general
*   history*
Geometrical and Mechanical Drawing;
*   Designing*
Shop Work—forging, welding, tempering,
*   soldering, braising, molding and casting;*
*   Proper care and use tools*

THIRD YEAR

Geometry (finished); Plane Trigonometry and
*   Mensuration.*
English Composition and Literature; Social
*   Science.*
Elements of Chemistry—laboratory work and
*   lectures; Principals of Mechanics.*
Bookkeeping.
Machine and Architectural Drawing; Designing.
Shop Work—bench work and fitting, turning,
*   drilling, planing, screw-cutting, etc.;*
*   study of the steam engine, including*
*   management and care of steam engines*
*   and boilers.*
Elementary Principals of the Textile and Fictile
*   Arts, Stone Work and Masonry.*
Instruction to be given in the properties of
*   materials—wood, iron, brass, clays, stone,*
*   wool, cotton, etc. throughout the course.*

On Tuesday, September 1, 1885, the Central Manual Training School opened in the old Hoffman School Building at Seventeenth and Wood. It was praised nationally for its efficiency and the high success rate of its students. By 1889, the modest building had proven insufficient for the student population, not to mention the machinery and technological workshops that a manual training school required. Calls for a new school soon began. The decision to create a second manual training school for the city resulted in the formation of the Northeast Manual Training School. It was decided to convert the twenty-six-year-old Lee Public School on Howard Street (below Girard) into the new school. Its location was in the general northeast quadrant of the still growing city proper.

Along with the first students who took their seats in September 1890 came the birth of the biggest school sibling rivalry in Philadelphia's history. During its first operating year, Northeast was immediately viewed as an unwanted little brother by Central, and the two manual training schools were soon in competition with each other. After many changes in location, title and student body, they are still rivals to this day. By 1910, the Southern Manual Training School was in operation in South Philadelphia, adding a third branch. Soon the manual training schools in the city became noted for their success, and their futures looked bright.

The sharp rise in population to river ward neighborhoods like Kensington and Fishtown at the turn of the century crammed hundreds of new students into Northeast. As early as 1901, school board members had been pushing for a new building of sufficient size. Northeast's principal, Andrew Morrison, needless to say, was one of the loudest voices in favor of a new school. Reform governor Samuel Pennypacker signed into law a bill that shifted the public school district from the old ward-based system—which allowed resident children from most wards to attend any school their parents desired—and put a modern parochial plan into structured use. Philadelphia Board of Education member Thomas Shallcross used his political connections to secure a site for the new Northeast. Being a resident of Northeast Philadelphia, Shallcross represented his district well.

In 1901, board of education architect J. Horace Cook—working with his assistant, Lloyd Titus—drew up plans for a Norman Gothic castle. Made of quarried stone and decorated with carved anvils, hammers and books, the new school peaked into a central tower rising

a story above the rest of the building. The one-hundred-foot tower spiked into four octagonal turrets, which were crowned by gargoyles, and the school almost alarmingly resembled a European castle or a medieval prison. After some bickering, the chosen site for the new building was one square block on the north side of Lehigh Avenue, between Seventh and Eighth Streets.

Ground was broken for the new school in 1903, in front of a wide-eyed neighborhood audience. It was completed two years later. Looking to make its opening as high profile as possible, the board called on President Theodore Roosevelt to perform an oration at the building's dedication. However, he declined due to "duty pressures." The board then turned to Princeton University president and future

U.S. president Dr. Woodrow Wilson, who proudly attended and orated the dedication. The *Evening Bulletin* reported on the opening:

> The building itself stands back from Lehigh Avenue a full seventy five feet, allowing a splendid view of its solid outlines and central tower. The construction of the building is simplicity itself, but it is admirably adapted to the use for which the school was designed. The building is three stories in height, and is built square around a courtyard in the center. On three sides the rooms face towards the outside, while the side hallways are lighted from the courtyard. On the north side, each floor is a single enormous room

This 1910 postcard shows the shining palace of education that Northeast Manual Training School was intended to be. Its design was considered one of the best in the country.

Morrison Hall—the large two-story auditorium
at Northeast—had more than seven hundred
seats. It was named for the school's first
principal, Dr. Andrew Morrison.

stretching from window to window. On the Lehigh Avenue front are the offices of administration and the classrooms of the academic departments of the school. On the eastern side, the laboratories of the scientific department rise one above another. On the western end, the assembly room occupies two sides, with the sky lighted drawing rooms above.

All the power for the various machines in the manual department is supplied from two great dynamos whose wires convey electricity to the motors which hang in the various rooms. These dynamos are run by two Corliss engines of a sufficiently simple type to enable the senior pupils to study their construction.

By 1910, Philadelphia's population was close to 2 million. The city's giant arms of social and political mobility, headed by its industrial hands and long, residential fingers, stretched farther north and west. A restructuring of the district plan was undertaken, and more new schools were built. In 1912, the school board, in response to fast-filling budget perimeters, consolidated the manual training schools with their regional district's academic high schools. The Central, Northeast, Southern and Western Manual Training Schools became simply Central High School, Northeast High School, South Philadelphia High School and so on. Although they still provided the same manual training curriculum as before, the focus of trade-based study was less blatant. As part of the same restructuring plan, the district high school policy was slightly revised. As listed in *A History of the Northeast High School, Philadelphia* by A.O. Michener, the new district alignments were as follows:

REQUIRED
Northeast—Between Allegheny Avenue and Susquehanna Avenue, east of the Schuylkill River.

OPTIONAL
Central or Northeast—Between Susquehanna Avenue and Montgomery Avenue, east of Schuylkill River.
Northeast or Frankford—Forty-fifth Ward, Thirty-third Ward, north of Allegheny Avenue.

Germantown or Northeast—Twenty-first Ward; Thirty-seventh, Thirty-eighth, and Forty-third Wards north of Allegheny Avenue. Germantown, Frankford or Northeast—Forty-second Ward.

During the First World War, many students in Philadelphia enlisted in the military or were drafted. Northeast lost almost half of its student body to the draft. Encouraged to fight by their principal, as in most high schools at the time, the boys of Northeast were sent off with a song by a patriotic Dr. Andrew Morrison:

Let every son of Northeast
His voice uplift in song.
That all may know her honor
Above all stain or wrong.
And when the strife is over,
And we are called to rest,
There still shall come forth others
Thy worth to manifest.

Just before the war, in September 1916, Morrison—along with school board member Thomas Shallcross and its vice-president, Simon Gratz—were able to gain an appropriation of $450,000 for expansions and improvements at Northeast. The war held up construction until 1919, when work began on two large additions. One was on the east side of the building facing Seventh Street, and the other was on the west side facing Eighth. In February 1920, the first of which—the large gymnasium on the east side, called Shallcross Hall—opened to a very excited class of freshmen. Later that year, Dr. Morrison passed away. His replacement was Dr. George Stradling, who oversaw the completion of the western addition—the large, decorative auditorium. Stradling saw to it that the magnificent new assembly hall, with seating for more than seven hundred, was named Morrison Hall for his friend and former colleague.

The middle-class community surrounding Northeast continued to fill up fast, and the school again became overcrowded. The new board appealed to the federal government for financial assistance in building another large addition. In 1935, the Federal Works Administration (a branch of the WPA) granted the board $414,000 of the needed $940,000 for new construction. By 1936, the remaining

No longer swarming with students, a classroom at Northeast appears frozen in time in this 2007 photo.

funds had been raised, and the project proceeded. Architect Ralph S. Herzog's Art Deco design for the four-story yellow brick annex contrasted with the old stone castle noticeably. It's façade fronted Somerset Street, attaching to the original structure's rear. Above the entrance was placed an artistic terra-cotta carving. The roof was encaged by fencing and used as an outdoor recreation area, as the original athletic yard, nicknamed "cinder park" by students, was taken up by the new addition.

The full-sized Northeast High School accommodated 1,500 students per year, and its rivalry with Central High expanded to sports. The two schools' football teams battled each other ferociously at every annual Thanksgiving Day game, a tradition that continues today. Beginning in the 1940s, the neighborhood around the school slowly diversified. Its

German majority was thinning out as the population escaped the crowded, unclean conditions of the city for the comforts and space of the developing neighborhoods of Northeast Philadelphia. Known as "white flight," this migration had led almost half of the neighborhood's population up to the "great northeast" by the late 1940s. In their place came eager working-class folks from other industrial neighborhoods, including African American and Irish families. Servicemen returning from the war found the old neighborhood crowded and more ethnically diverse than when they left and followed the pattern of relocation to the northeast. Their speedy departure caused property values to drop.

By 1950, the predominant white middle class made up just over half of the area's population. Northeast High had not necessarily lost any of its quality education standards or any of its revered specialty training accolades. Unfortunately, like many cities at a time before civil rights, Philadelphia's "brotherly love" was conditional, and restrictions did apply. As early as 1951, talk loomed among school board members about a way to "handle the situation" at Northeast. In an attempt to "save the school's reputation," the school district would build a new school in a new community. Its stated reasoning, which one could say is quite logical, was that the new school was built to serve the new and quickly expanding communities in the northeast section of the city. Sensibly, the new communities were to the northeast of the old school, and therefore a new Northeast High School was needed. But an all-too-clear pattern of systematic prejudice was not hard to link to the city's move.

In 1953, the experienced engineering and architectural firm of Ballinger & Company, which also constructed Budd's Hunting Park plant, received the contract for the new school to be located on Cottman Avenue, between Algon and Summerdale Avenues. The ultramodern school took advantage of the abundance of open space that the northeast provided. Instead of stacking its floors and using its roof as an exercise yard, the new building itself sprawled out over ten acres. Its grounds took up an impressive one hundred acres, containing several baseball fields and a runners' track. By the time the new building opened in 1957, the school district had already been the focus of criticism and anger over the move. Parents who were Northeast alumni themselves and wanted their boys to attend the school complained to the school district and city hall.

On February 1, 1957, Northeast High School's five-decade trophy collection was taken from the building at Eighth and Lehigh and put on display in the new school, which was receiving its first graduating class. The last piece of the old school's identity—its name—was finally removed and given to the new building on Cottman Avenue. The formidable old castle of learning on Lehigh was given the new title: Thomas A. Edison High School. In November 1957, its principal, Robert Wayne Clark, issued a pamphlet to its students, faculty and parents entitled *A Report to Our Community*. In it, Clark attempted to emphasize the importance of the old building and its unchanged faculty. His positive words helped boost the morale of the downed school:

We believe our community will agree that the change in name is the only significant change that has taken place. Whether we are right in this belief or not, we want our community to know exactly what Edison is and exactly what Edison offers our boys. Here at Eighth and Lehigh, the new school will occupy one of the most beautiful—if one of the older—of Philadelphia's school buildings—a building rich in the fine tradition which has grown up through almost seventy years of educational service to Philadelphia boys. It is true the Northeast name has been taken away and the name Thomas A. Edison will soon appear over the entrance; but the spirit and the tradition are as inseparable parts of this location as are the stones, the stained-glass windows, the high fretted ceilings and the quiet, cool corridors of the old building.

The boys of the Edison community lift their heads with a new pride in the certainty that a good world is theirs— that they need only claim it through the process of hard work. Already this process has begun. When the first consciousness of the loss of an ancient and respected name left them bewildered, the boys reacted as boys are likely to do when they are deprived without what they consider good reason. In their disappointment some of the upper classmen fixed their eyes on the Northeast name and tried to the end to keep the association which was denied to them. In closing, the pangs of birth— while sharp—are short, and Edison High School is today a new, independent and proud institution saluting the community it serves.

The Thomas Edison High School did indeed keep up its stellar tradition of higher learning and quickly developed its own identity. However, the days of battling Central High for the unofficial "best of Philly" status were over, and Edison's secondhand crown of acclaim was certainly lighter. Its ethnically polarized yet oddly unified student body of middle-class boys maintained the status quo, although racial disparity played an

The tall institutional hallways of Northeast began their state of water-induced decay shortly after the theft of its copper roof exhaust fans. In this 2010 photo, colorful graffiti stubbornly demands to be noticed.

Philly's skyline stands tall over the rotting remains of Northeast in 2012. The school's gargoyle-studded medieval turrets contrast boldly against the ever-progressing urban landscape.

This 2014 photo shows the current state of Northeast. The original portion has been demolished, but the 1936 Herzog addition is to be integrated into public housing.

obvious part in the school's stained reputation. Nonetheless, Edison's students continued to represent the city's educational opportunities well, and the school did its best to hold on to its inherent strengths.

By the 1960s, Edison was feeling the squeeze as a true inner-city school. With a population of almost 2,400 students and nearly 80 faculty members, the building was pushing its limits. Amid the civil rights battles of the 1960s, however, Edison pulled

through comparatively well. As the community endured more sweeping ethnic and sociopolitical changes, Edison's student body became even more intricately diversified. Waves of Latino immigrants—mostly from Puerto Rico—flooded into the yet again deserted neighborhoods of Fairhill and West Kensington, surrounding Edison. By 1970, the waves had become deluges, and the city literally did not have enough schools in the area to send the new

immigrant children, most of whom spoke no English.

A "temporary" solution was put in place by converting a number of vacant textile mills and factories into schools. One example is the Roberto Clemente Middle School, which was converted from the seven-story Apex Hosiery Company building at Fifth and Luzerne Streets. Meant only to act as a school until the city built a proper structure for the now swarming immigrant districts, Clemente Middle School—despite its asbestos content and insufficient building features—remained in operation until the late 1990s. As the property value in the area continued to decline, more African American and Latino families relocated there. The neighborhood soon became one of the city's highest crime districts.

In the mid-1970s, the Frank Rizzo administration took up the effort of demolishing "every last one" of Philadelphia's estimated 100,000 abandoned row homes. Focusing on high crime areas, Rizzo narrowed in on the connected wards of West Kensington, Fairhill, Hunting Park, Franklinville and Harrowgate. His administration demolished roughly 10,000 vacant row homes in North Philadelphia. However, with no immediate plans to replace the homes, the result was an ugly, barren landscape speckled with crime, trash and graffiti. By the late 1970s, the area had become unofficially known as the "Badlands," owing to both its desolate environment and high crime rate. The Badlands—needless to say—quickly became an emporium for drugs and guns. Its powerful street gangs became a threatening opponent of the Philadelphia Police Department, and its overwhelming status as a drug market would only expand, making it one of the most dangerous neighborhoods in North America by the 1990s.

By 1979, Edison had finally become coed and was operating over capacity. A sad statistic calculated after the close of the Vietnam War showed that Edison had the highest alumni death count of any high school in America. Fifty-four of its students lost their lives in the war. The 1980s continued the push of more dangerous students into Edison, and its status as a school was on a steady decline. The faculty, too, had diminished. The once proud learning center was now stuffed to the brim, behind on maintenance and increasingly incapable of dealing with the prevalent crime and violence. By 1986, a new Edison High was in the works. Situated on what was once the grounds of the Philadelphia Municipal Hospital for Contagious Diseases at Second and Luzerne Streets, the new Thomas A. Edison High School opened in 1988 and is still in use today.

The tired old structure at Eighth and Lehigh was cleaned out and locked up. It sat until the mid-1990s, when the Julia de Burgos Bi-Lingual Middle Magnet School—a private charter school—began its lease of the building, which was named for the famous Puerto Rican poet. The administration of De Burgos was able to perform enough maintenance to get the school up to building code standards. As its third incarnation, the building served the overwhelmingly Hispanic population, teaching basic courses, as well as specialty studies geared toward adapting to American life. In 2002, the old building no longer met the necessary public building safety codes, and the required repairs were far too costly. Thus, it was closed forever. A new Julia de Burgos was built just two blocks east and was in use by 2003. The old Northeast/Edison, again owned by the school district, was sealed up and locked down in 2003.

Surprisingly, given its location, the building remained remarkably non-vandalized until about 2007, when it was finally discovered by scrappers. The cash-strapped school district was unable to properly maintain security of the square-block property, and before long, its precious metals had disappeared, including the copper exhaust fans on the roof. Water quickly infiltrated the holes, destabilizing the old building's wooden roof support beams, and began its thorough destruction of the one-hundred-year-old landmark. Squatters and addicts soon took up residence in the school. Two corpses were removed from the building by police in 2008. Animals had scattered the remains of one across two separate floors by the time it was located. The surrounding community became concerned with the presence of the increasingly dangerous (not to mention scary-looking) castle of decadence, and police presence became more frequent.

By 2011, the neighborhood, working closely with city officials, had agreed on a plan for the property's reuse. However, financial constraints held up demolition for another year and a half, during which time a crippling fire took out the original building's wooden roof and top floor. Demolition of the tired, scarred old landmark

finally commenced in 2013. Today, the site's new owners—Mosaic Development Partners and Orens Brothers Real Estate—are in the process of constructing the Edison Square shopping center. Their clever concept calls for the rehabilitation of the 1936 Herzog rear addition into apartments. The cornerstone of the original building was transferred to the current Northeast on Cottman Avenue and placed among its rightful namesake. Although its scowling gargoyles no longer pierce Philly's skyline, its elegant auditorium no longer hosts national dignitaries and the medieval gray stones of its façade no longer instill the seriousness of good education into new generations, the old Northeast High School will remain in the halls of Philadelphia's distinct history forever.

CHAPTER 4

FINANCE

For more than two centuries, the City of Brotherly Love has embodied a sense of neighborhood hospitality that has often been regarded as unique. It is aptly named for a reason. The way the city's planners followed the founder's general idea of community-rich relations truly shows in the patterned row homes and corner stores of the streetcar neighborhoods. These factors combined to create a habitat for social mobility. A little imagination conjures up a block full of happy middle-class residents. Some are sweeping off their front steps, while others are perched out upstairs windows, their arms crossed as they survey the activity on their block.

The changing environment of the growing city was getting only more complex. But Philadelphians liked it that way. They never had to stray far to shop, eat, work or play. The "walking" city was easier to navigate before the age of the automobile, and the sense of commonality was stronger. The rise of the streetcars provided access to new residential areas and sculpted the layout of the present city. The "streetcar suburbs" forced businesses to expand as well. In some cases, being pushed farther out of the city by the growing neighborhoods ended up being a blessing to businesses by necessitating outreach. Philadelphia's banking firms, however, some of the oldest in the country, had become the true backbone of the city by the end of the Civil War.

As the multitudes of new industries developed innovative technologies that made Philadelphia the manufacturing mecca of the nineteenth century, the second and third generations of the city's hierarchal banking aristocracy found themselves in almost invincible positions. Firms like the Philadelphia Savings Fund Society (PSFS), the Philadelphia National Bank (PNB) and Guarantee Safe and Trust Company kept their management and ownership within their own tightknit financial families. Those who controlled Philadelphia's money would, in turn, control its businesses and then its government. The banks' strong hold on Philadelphia would last until the mid-twentieth century, when they were legally disbanded, along with their many branches of effect, such as the utility companies. This chapter will focus on two financial firms that remain—in body only—in Philadelphia.

Keystone National Bank/ Hale Building

PERHAPS TODAY, PHILADELPHIA can be defined by fine architecture and grand, monolithic structures like city hall. Its modern skyscrapers neatly shape its unique skyline, and its iconic monumental buildings like Independence Hall and the Art Museum are known worldwide. But back in the age of social and technological experimentation, Philadelphians' ideas of tasteful architecture were quite skewed. The roughly laid framework of the city's government after the Civil War, combined with its unprecedented corruption, may have lent Philadelphia the appearance of a city with some weird priorities. Compared to other cities that existed during the period of Reconstruction following the Civil War, Philadelphia had an almost unique role. Its long-stretched family bloodlines had, for almost two centuries, been digging the city's roots deep, and a solid system of banks, businesses and bureaucracy seemed to only strengthen after the war.

There was comparatively little social reconstruction kicking off in the City of Brotherly Love after the bloodiest war Americans had yet seen. The Quaker City had always maintained a sober, plain look in its buildings and houses. The Friends were strongly against extreme wealth and believed in penitence and humble uniformity. Therefore, Philadelphia's architecture remained very modest, and its red brick houses and factories created a drab maze. However, from the malaise in which Philadelphia found itself during the years following Lincoln's famous funeral procession, a daring new form of architecture was born. It would be a refreshing slap in the face to the dull architecture of the city.

Drafting student Frank Furness was the youngest son of a Unitarian minister. His upbringing in

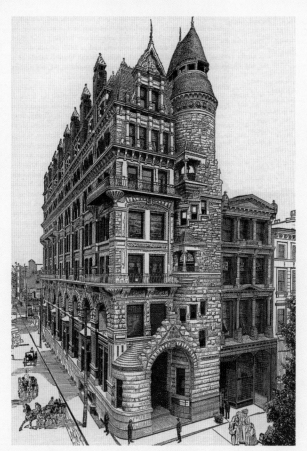

RIGHT This picturesque 1887 drawing shows the Hale Building before its southward expansion to Sansom Street. The city's busy Victorian financial district once rivaled Wall Street. *Courtesy the Athenaeum of Philadelphia.*

OPPOSITE Although heavily altered at its street level façade, the upper floors of the Hale Building remain in mostly original condition, inside and out.

In the 1890s—before the age of the skyscraper—this perspective from Hale's fifth-floor front office would have revealed quite a view, overlooking Wanamaker's Grand Depot.

Philadelphia made the aspiring designer well aware of its architectural void. When Furness returned from the Civil War, however, he was a focused and humorless man. He became a student and assistant to eclectic New York architect Richard Morris Hunt. But after his training, Furness came home to Philadelphia with big lessons to teach, as well as a few to learn. Through his recent war experiences, his frustration with the old Quaker powers that controlled the city's building projects and his outlandish and unapologetic personality, Furness changed Philadelphia architecture forever. His totally unique style, called "Furnessque" by his critics, was a wild, satirical caricature of traditional architectural forms such as Gothic or Queen Anne. Furness threw them all into his designs, while adding his own touches. His buildings broke almost every architectural ethic and showed Philadelphia his anger with its customs. He once commented on his strong desire to gather together all of his clients at the Academy of Music so he could "get up on stage and tell them all to go to Hell." Sadly, today most of his work is demolished.

Furness did manage, however, to start a small local cult following of sorts among other living architects of his day. Brewery architect Otto Wolf designed a bank that still sits on the corner of Ridge and Girard Avenues that smacked so strongly of Furness that his own office had difficulty denying involvement in it. Another architect who rose on the coattails of Furness's architectural reign was Willis Gaylord Hale. Hale's buildings definitely display the love of disorganization apparent in Furness's designs while also maintaining their own identity. His love of the Queen Anne style shows in the many mansions he designed for Philadelphia's elite, most of which still survive in the Chestnut Hill area. Hale's contracts came through the political and business connections he'd managed to acquire. Many came from his friends in the financial district of Chestnut Street. One of Hale's few surviving commercial buildings is the Keystone National Bank (Hale Building) on the southwest corner of Juniper and Chestnut Streets. What's left of its erratic façade stands out amid its modern neighbors.

In 1886, Hale received the commission for the new bank in the heart of the city's booming financial district, and the building was completed one year later. The original structure, under the title of the Lucas Building (named for the bank's former president), extended only to Drury Street. It featured a raised first floor that contained a very colorful lobby and teller area. In 1890, the building was extended to Sansom Street, reaching its current size. Its Chestnut Street façade, made of rock-faced Indiana limestone, shows a sense of aggravation that many architects of the period were experiencing. Furness's bold new style was simply an easy path to follow, allowing for a reason to break out of the restraints of Philadelphia's dull prison of architectural plainness.

Having survived the financial panic of the 1880s, the Keystone National Bank was considered a stable institution. One of its biggest depositors was the city government, which entrusted the bank with an unusually heavy $300,000 per year. Therefore, it came as a shock when the bank suddenly collapsed in 1891. An investigation showed that hundreds of thousands of dollars were missing, along with the bank's president, Gideon W. Marsh, who could not be located for questioning. It also showed that the bank had become a front for the "City Hall Gang" (or simply "the Gang"), a faction of Republican ward bosses and city councilmen that had controlled Philadelphia politics for decades.

By 1892, the investigation of Keystone National Bank had dug painfully deep into the Gang's corrupt and complicated system of graft. Several arrests were finally made, including that of City Treasurer John Bardsley, most likely the Gang's "fall guy," who was served seventeen indictments and a stiff prison sentence. Meanwhile, bank president Marsh was still nowhere to be found. In fact, more than seven years passed before his eventual surrender in 1898. By that time, the calculations were solid. When all was said and done, the Gang had siphoned off about $1.5 million from the taxpayers of Philadelphia through the Keystone National Bank. Lippincott's publication *Philadelphia and Its Environs* called the Keystone scandal "a defalcation of and an abuse of public trust not likely soon to be forgotten in the annals of the Quaker City."

Disassociating itself from the Keystone Bank, the new building owners—the Central Savings Fund, Trust and Safe Deposit Company— changed its name to the Hale Building, after its architect. Hale's architectural firm moved into the building soon after. It included several notable

Stabbing red paint and a gaudy light fixture are stains of the Hale's later years as various offices.

architects, such as Angus Wade. The budding architectural practice, although short-lived, was very productive and highly successful. Hale's flagship building, the Lorraine Apartments (Divine Lorraine Hotel), was conceptualized and drawn up there in 1892. Sadly, a fire at the office claimed just about all of Hale's designs in 1896, bankrupting the architect, and he died of diabetes (and almost destitute) in 1907. Several other members of the firm carried on their own practices at the Hale Building for roughly another decade. By the 1930s, the building housed an array of tenants including detective agencies, insurance companies and, eventually, department stores. By the 1940s, most of the upper floors were vacant. In the 1950s, the New York clothing chain Franklin Simon purchased the building and converted it into a store. This resulted in the loss of the entire first-floor exterior façade. It was covered in favor of a more modern look, contrasting loudly with the rest of the building's Victorian eclecticism. Its raised rooftop cupola was also removed in the 1950s, when a second elevator was installed.

In the 1980s, the short-lived Bellevue Health Spa occupied the fourth floor, offering saunas, steam rooms, gyms and personal training. However, it soon became notorious as an unofficial gathering place for homosexuals, who had been regentrifying the area since the late 1970s. Bellevue was closed in the late 1980s after the discovery of HIV and AIDS put an end to the open sexual behavior that had apparently been taking place there. In the 1990s, the first floor became occupied by a discount store, which operated until 2011. In 2009, a developer submitted solid plans to convert the building into condominiums featuring a ground-floor restaurant and bar. This plan seems to have been discarded, and today the building is vacant, awaiting restoration. Hopefully the rarity of this architectural beauty will not be overlooked. As the last of the eclectic Victorian banks, the Hale shows off the undeniable power with which Philadelphia's financial institutions held sway over its government. With luck, it will survive for future generations to behold.

National Bank of North Philadelphia/Beury Building

A DRIVER OR PASSENGER traveling Broad Street—Philadelphia's main artery—is forced to notice the presence of a tall, disarrayed structure boldly displaying the phrase "boner forever" vertically down its ribcage. Where Broad Street meets Erie Avenue, the eye-catching rot of the tallest building for half a square mile sprouts up from its concrete soil. Every window has been removed, and air rushes through the building like a screen door. The caved-in roof exposes the building's interior to the elements, and it can be seen for blocks in every direction, sticking up like a middle finger. It's a message to the new generation, whose parents and grandparents fled the inner city and let this shining tower crumble into a dangerous eyesore. An erratic mess of Art Deco architecture, graffiti and building decay marks the place where middle-class families of the once thriving neighborhood of Franklinville stored their money for safekeeping.

The financial district around the intersection of Broad and Erie was a budding one in the mid-1920s. This predominantly Irish Catholic neighborhood, known as Franklinville, was an up-and-coming community. Evidence of the area's prewar majesty can be seen in the large and elegant four-story "row mansions" that still line Franklinville's main streets of Erie and Allegheny Avenues. The area already contained several successful banks. But in 1925, amid the slowly cresting wave of American economic combustion, architect William Harold Lee received the contract for the new fourteen-story bank tower of the National Bank of North Philadelphia. In a bold attempt to mark the rising new district, Lee would design one of Philadelphia's best examples of Art Deco architecture. Lee is known for designing the elegant Conwell Hall at Temple University, as well as several theaters in the Philadelphia area. The National Bank of North Philadelphia, a brazen young firm, clearly did not see any cracks in the shining economy. Its million-dollar skyscraper, the company hoped, would be the easy start of a new financial epicenter, and other banks would follow its lead.

Lee's design for the building spared little expense in its expression of safety and permanence. Yet the mechanized look of the new Art Deco movement, mostly popular in Europe in these early years, appeared subtler than eclectic Victorian bank designs, such as the Keystone or Furness's Guarantee Safe and Trust Company. Lee's main lobby was lined with imported marble and crystal chandeliers. On the exterior, the raised first floor was highlighted in limestone from the rest of the brick structure. The look of the fourteen-story tower was years ahead of its time. Lee's future work would move almost completely into the Art Deco style. This new building a half century later would be hailed by architectural critics as the first Art Deco skyscraper in Philadelphia, although the Philadelphia Savings Fund Society (PSFS) building on Market Street holds the official title.

At the head of the National Bank of North Philadelphia was its outspoken president, Dr. Charles Ezra Beury. Beury (pronounced "berry") was the second president of Temple University, as well as of several newly formed banks and trust companies,

The National Bank of North Philadelphia, known as the Beury Building, towers fourteen stories over busy Broad Street. The firm had hoped that its skyscraper would attract other financial institutions to the area, which its members helped develop.

and he was a key figure in organizing the new banking district along north Broad Street. Using his network of other young investors, such as future Philadelphia commerce baron Albert Greenfield, Beury was determined to lead his new bank to the top, next to Philadelphia's prominent Chestnut Street banks. Within just a few years of its opening, the building came to officially bear his name—the Beury Building. The 1920s were very busy years in the financial sector, and patronage at the Beury Building was high.

In 1928, the National Bank of North Philadelphia merged with several other firms under the umbrella of the Philadelphia Banker's Trust Company, whose board included Beury, Greenfield and other future successful Philadelphia bankers. Seen even by financial experts to be too big to fail, the Bankers Trust Company had just gotten on its feet with four other banks under its ownership, and had almost $50 million in deposits, when the Wall Street crash of 1929 sent the bank toppling down hard. In 1930, the bank turned its operations over to the state and never reopened.

Although beaten and bruised, Beury was far from defeated. His varied business interests provided enough stability to allow him to rebuild his bank. With help from colleagues like Greenfield, Beury climbed back into the shaky financial world. Although his efforts were strong, Beury's banks could not heal the damage from the Great Depression, and they would never again see a profit. Like many other bank owners after the Wall Street crash, Beury began living differently. He devoted his professional efforts to his trust companies, some of which had barely survived the crash. But Dr. Beury put most of his time into his presidency of Temple University.

In 1933, Beury spoke of the financial crash to students at Chester Military College. According to Beury, "wild speculation and allowing the reins of government to be handled by selfish politicians" was the cause of the "economic chaos" that prevailed. "Perhaps the present plight of the American people will bring them back to the principal laid down by the founders of the nation," he said. "It certainly will chase them away from the worship of the dollar." Beury continued as the president of Temple University until 1941. He died in 1953 and was buried in his family plot, where he rests among many other prominent Philadelphia figures, at Laurel Hill Cemetery. The fate of the Beury Building was up in the air for several years after the Second World War, with its smaller clientele holding the building together. But more than half of its offices were unoccupied. It began to fill up in the 1950s, and its floors hosted medical, law and real estate offices, as well as branches of other companies and local institutions.

"White flight" began in the 1960s, transforming Beury's surrounding landscape. By the 1970s, Beury's tenants had almost all vacated the building, and beginning with its upper floors, abandonment slowly set in. Without maintenance, the fourteen-story tower began to wither. Its plaster walls and ceilings became gradually infiltrated by rainwater, revealing innards of flaking asbestos, which sealed the building's fate and ensured that its offices would remain empty. Recognized as one of Philadelphia's premier Art Deco works, the vacant building was added to the National Historic Register in 1985. Although a few other adaptive reuse attempts were proposed, the increasing ferocity of crime in the area kept developers away.

In 1987, Muhammed Mizani—a shady local property investor—acquired the building under a move by the city to sell off its blighted properties. Mizani owned a number of properties in

Beury's scarred face displays the look of sad longing for a bygone chapter of a complicated city. The Art Deco bank can be seen for miles.

the city, including several homeless shelters and drug rehab centers. He purchased the Beury cheaply, under the condition that he would assume all cleanup costs, including $250,000 for the structure's abatement. Beginning in 1988, Mizani organized an extremely low-cost labor force consisting of homeless addicts from his other properties and put them to work removing the deadly asbestos. In a clear violation of the Clean Air Act, Mizani's workers removed hundreds of pounds worth of the cancer-causing fiber from the first floor and disposed of it illegally. However, a visiting city inspector served Mizani with a warning after only a few months, and the process supposedly stopped.

By 1991, however, it had become clear that the illegal removal of the asbestos was continuing, as more workers from Mizani's shelter at Twelfth and Vine commenced the cleaning of the higher floors. Another surprise visit by city inspectors in 1992 produced photos of men working without proper safety equipment, and some with none at all. When the photos reached Environmental Protection Agency officials in D.C., a federal investigation into Mizani began. The Federal Bureau of Investigation finally indicted Mizani and three other workers in November 1994. The sixty-year-old maintained his innocence, claiming that he was not aware of the working conditions. He told the judge that he was the victim of a conspiracy and that he was being unjustly prosecuted because he was Muslim. Mizani's attorney aggressively insisted that the allegations against his client could never be proven. But thirty-three-year-old William Waters, a tenant in one of Mizani's halfway houses, acted as the prosecution's key witness. He claimed that he was offered to gather men for the job by Mizani and was willing to testify.

In 1995, Waters was found dead in his home with a gunshot wound to the chest, and the only witness that could link Mizani to the illegal work was gone. U.S. attorney Christopher Hall was aggravated but not defeated, and he pressed his case, bringing to light Mizani's entire crooked history. Mizani, however, did not seem worried. But when the prosecution played a secretly recorded phone call between Mizani and a city air quality inspector in which he denied ownership of the Beury Building, the case against him became damning. After exhausting every legal option he had, Mizani finally pleaded guilty in 1996, after learning that his three co-defendants had made a deal with Hall and were planning on testifying against him. He was sentenced to eighteen months in federal prison, and the Beury Building was put up for sale at sheriff's auction the following year.

Today, more talk of efforts to rehabilitate the ninety-year-old landmark appears in the local news, but so far nothing has been started. The upper floors of the building are dangerously exposed and structurally unsound. Scaffolding along the building's frontage on Broad Street and along its north siding on Airdrie Avenue directs foot traffic under a protective ceiling of plywood, since pieces if its rotting brick and terra-cotta flesh occasionally fall to the sidewalk below. Known sometimes as the "Boner Forever" building, old Beury is one of Philadelphia's most well-known ruins and still attracts visitors. Hopefully, a serious plan of rehabilitation will breathe new life into this beacon of North Philadelphia history.

CHAPTER 5

MILITARY

From the mind of Philadelphia's pacifist founder, William Penn, came a city unlike any in the world. A city that was intolerant to indifference, poverty and inequality. A clean, modern city with buildings built of brick that no great fire could destroy (like London in 1666). In Penn's dream of a place where any and all were welcome to live and, most importantly, practice any religion they chose, Philadelphia was a city that had no need for defenses. After all, who would seek to harm the people of such a unified society? Unfortunately, Penn's dream was a bit too perfect. Shortly after the arrival of its first settlers, conflicts began with Leni-Lenape Indians and Swedes, as well as infighting between colonists. Since the days of Penn's proprietorship, talk of protecting and defending the city from attack was very adamant among the colony's leading men. Contrasting views on the issue extended debates and prolonged any actual progress for half a century. To the Quaker City, defense and militarization were not priorities.

Philadelphia saw little military activity until the mid-eighteenth century, when Fort Mifflin was erected by the British to defend Philadelphia from French warships. By the close of the French and Indian War, Penn's anomalistic city was just like any other in the civilized world, and proper defenses proved a necessity. As Philadelphia became one of the largest cities in the nation, it would gain within its borders several military facilities, including the Frankford Arsenal, the Schuylkill Arsenal, the enormous Naval Shipyard at League Island, the U.S. Naval Quartermaster Depot and others. Thus, throughout the twentieth century, Philadelphia had a very intimate relationship with the defense of the nation, and its facilities can be credited with lending a strong portion of weight to America's superior military muscle. This chapter will focus on the remains of two of the city's important military facilities.

This aerial view of the Frankford Arsenal during demolition in 2010 shows about half of its clustered campus. The Crane Hospital can be seen near the upper right, shortly before its removal.

Frankford Arsenal

SITUATED ALONG THE NORTHERN branch of the Frankford Creek, near its mouth at the Delaware River, sits about 150 acres of some of the Philadelphia area's most historically neglected, though vitally significant, quadrants. The *Philadelphia Daily News* reported in 1991 that "at one time, Philadelphia's Frankford Arsenal was called *The Street that Beat Hitler* because every round of small ammunition fired in World War II [by U.S. troops] was made there." Today, the mighty Frankford Arsenal has been reduced to about a quarter of what it once encompassed. The area known as Frankford can be traced to Peter Rambo, a Swedish settler who acquired the land in about 1668. It was established about thirteen years later by Quakers from England. Over the years, the land changed hands many times, and in 1742, as part of a patent from John, Thomas and Richard Penn, grandsons of the founder, the land was given to Andrew Hamilton, builder of the statehouse (Independence Hall), who sold off the land over time.

After the Revolutionary War, when Philadelphia was briefly the nation's capital, new ideas concerning the city's defense were in wild dispute among Philadelphians. Pacifist Quakers had lost their political clout after refusing to participate in the war, and the new government seemed to plow in like a steamroller. But even in Congress, there were many who expressed antiwar sentiments, and getting the framework laid for facilities for a new military would prove a slow process. The Schuylkill Arsenal was established in about 1805 on the east bank of the Schuylkill River (near the Grays Ferry Avenue bridge) to provide a guarded location for the storage of muskets and ammunition for the country's military force. At roughly the same time, the formation of an administrative body to oversee these small weapons caches—the U.S. Army Ordnance Department—was completed, and the roots of the country's young arsenal system were finding their place.

The War of 1812 brought on a strong attitude shift concerning militarization. In 1816, Congress approved a bill for purchase of land for a new United States Arsenal. The property of Fredrick Fraley on the bank of the Frankford Creek near the Delaware River was offered to the military for $7,680.75. Despite the antiwar sentiment of Frankford residents, Captain Joseph H. Rees—representing the U.S. Army Ordnance Department—purchased the twenty-two-acre parcel on May 27, 1816. One year later, former president James Madison attended the official dedication of the arsenal, and a cornerstone was laid on its first building, the west storehouse. With the completion of the west storehouse in 1817, the arsenal was put into operation.

The Ordnance Department, although considered insignificant by most U.S. Army officials, pushed for bigger budget appropriations and more employees. Life and work at the arsenal remained meager and menial, however, and general feelings toward the department remained negative. Some officials claimed that there was never a use for such a department and that it was a financial waste. Others called for the department's closure or reorganization. Yet despite all its opposition, the Ordnance Department would prove invaluable to America's armed forces. Determined to make purposeful its role in the new military legacy, the department continued calling for more duties and appropriations. Usually these calls fell on deaf ears. The U.S. military had been manufacturing most of its own small arms, muskets and rifles at its armories in Springfield, Massachusetts, and Harper's Ferry, Virginia, for decades. Officials were not anxious to expand these manufactories to other areas, partly due to local politics and shaky finances. Roughly 25 percent of the government's small arms, however, were acquired through a messy contract system.

Under this system, the Ordnance Department would receive a sample of a musket, rifle or projectile, as well as the precise measurements and gauging to be used to re-create the item as uniformly as possible. It was then the job of Ordnance to seek out a local arms manufacturer, exchange information with it and hire it to produce a given number of items. Ordnance would receive orders such as "twenty-five hundred muskets to be delivered within five years." It was then up to Ordnance to inspect the items and put them through very specific gauging, measurement and weight checks. If an item passed, it was taken to the west storehouse for shipment. If not, it was modified at the arsenal by Ordnance and rechecked until acceptable. It did not take long for the system to cause frustration and political rivalries on the surface. However, it also paved the way for the continued practice of American arms outsourcing. Private manufacturers such as the Fox Foundry and the Wickham Manufacturing Company were delighted by the contract system; they thrived under it, almost never running out of work. But among Ordnance and army officials,

bad blood was brewing. Captain Rees continued as arsenal commander, carrying on the contract system.

The endless repetitious act of measuring and gauging fortunately gave way to new innovations. The practice of working over and over with the same specific product eventually made its identification second nature. Arsenal armorers and metalworkers came up with new ideas, such as interchangeable, mass-produced, uniform parts. Rather than manufacturing an entire musket, a contractor could simply produce barrels or stocks. This gave the arsenal its first break in job function, and a continually growing shift in attitudes in favor of production at the arsenal would prove to be its future. New land purchases expanded the arsenal property, and new buildings were added.

By the 1820s, the arsenal's contractor base had reached out into several other states. Frequent business with the Du Pont Company of Delaware for powder also extended the arsenal's reach. It produced thousands of musket balls, hand-rolled them through brown paper for shape and then placed them into wrapped cartridges with 30 to 110 grains of gunpowder. These early paper cartridges, needless to say, were dangerous and inaccurate. The 1830s brought on the presidency of Andrew Jackson and, with it, a big boost to the nation's military. At the arsenal, increasing bureaucracy within the Ordnance Department brought several short-lived commanders through the facility. The early 1830s also saw the beginning of hired civilian labor at the arsenal.

In 1832, Colonel William J. Worth became the new arsenal commander. Worth desired an independent Ordnance Department, free from the control of the brass. This became a reality, and Worth called for all arsenal supplies existing in other facilities to be moved to the Frankford Arsenal. Having flooded several times, the Schuylkill Arsenal was losing its appeal as a stronghold. Worth had seen the Frankford Arsenal's location rise on the government's priority list due to location, size and management. He was soon able to arrange an official procedural change that required *all* of the Ordnance Department's powder be proved at the arsenal. In 1833, Worth's request for $5,778.79 for "the erection of two brick buildings, each forty feet long and nineteen feet wide," was approved by Congress, and the

arsenal received its first new buildings in almost two decades.

Worth pushed further, and in 1834, another $16,170 was granted for a three-story building "120' x 40,' of brick and stone." With only twenty-five workers, however, Worth knew that he needed more. He pressed for an additional ten workers but was denied by Colonel Bomford of Ordnance. Whether Worth wore out his welcome with his constant requests is a curious point. In January 1835, he was ordered by Bomford to turn over command of the arsenal to Captain Alfred Mordecai, a top-of-his-class West Point graduate of 1823 and a devoted student of science who, to Bomford's dismay, welcomed the Industrial Revolution to the Frankford Arsenal. Worth

would achieve fame in the Mexican-American War before dying of cholera in 1849. Today, he is buried beneath his large monument at Worth Square in Manhattan.

After impressing the brass with his leadership as commander of the Washington Arsenal, Alfred Mordecai was a great choice as commander at Frankford. During his three years in charge, he accomplished a great deal at the arsenal. He oversaw the completion of the east storehouse and the laboratory, had the entire property's roads re-graveled and planted the accent trees surrounding the freshly completed parade grounds. He also had a bulkhead erected along the Frankford Creek to prevent the property from flooding. Mordecai had an interest

Old cannons—captured during the Spanish-American War—neatly flank the entrance to one of many buildings at Frankford Arsenal erected for the First World War.

The 1852 percussion cap factory was fortunate enough to survive the demolition of half of the campus in 2012. The tiny building was the arsenal's first step toward its role as a military production giant.

in the geography of the arsenal and took it upon himself to both bulk up and beautify the developing military installation.

In 1836, the property was expanded to the east again with the purchase and absorption of the former Kennedy property, and a protective seven-foot stone wall was erected along the new eastern edge. It still stands today. Two years later, Mordecai was reassigned to the Ordnance office in Washington, D.C. Replacing him as commander of the arsenal was Captain George Douglas Ramsay, who had rather different ideas on how the arsenal should function. Ramsay was also a West Point graduate and had served with both the Corps of Light Artillery and the Corps of Topographical Engineers. The financial depression of 1837 took away some of the arsenal's enlisted men, and with them went other civilian jobs. It slowly recovered, however, in the years following.

By the time the Kensington riots of 1844 came a bit too close for comfort for the arsenal, it was almost undefended. Ramsay wrote to the Ordnance Department with a request for arms and soldiers after he was notified by the sheriff of Philadelphia County, Morton McMichael, that "there is a rumor that rioters intend to attack the Arsenal and the Catholic Church at Frankford." They never did, but the Mexican-American War soon got the arsenal moving at a steady pace again. Although a decent commander, Ramsay never seemed to much enjoy his post at the arsenal. He left for Texas to join Company K in 1845, seeing combat as his only chance for advancement away from the monotonous administration of the Frankford Arsenal.

Taking Ramsay's place as arsenal commander was former second lieutenant Andrew Dearborn. The young new commander was immediately faced with a sharp rise in orders for gunpowder and ammunition to fight the unpopular Mexican-American War. To meet the demand, the arsenal hired a larger workforce than it ever had previously. Dearborn warned the Ordnance Department that the area surrounding the arsenal was rapidly becoming populated by factories and industrial sites. He recommended the quick purchase of more adjacent land before it was sold, stressing that "these manufactories do not come singly, but in crowds." But the Ordnance Department was unresponsive.

At the close of the war in 1849, George Ramsay, now a major, seemed happy to return to his quiet position of arsenal commander. Upon his reappointment, the Ordnance Department approved $20,000 for the purchase of the adjacent Ashmead property. The Ordnance Department must have learned a few lessons from the Mexican-American War, as much more interest was put into the idea of mass production and the scientific study of ammunition manufacture. With the birth of American industrialism, the concept of technological advancement was finally introduced to the arms production trade, and the military-industrial complex began to form.

The 1850s saw the Ordnance Department's ideals of uniformity and specificity of product start on their way to perfection. The department began to find its place as a true government entity, developing its modus operandi and pioneering the practice of complete standardization for all its manufactured goods. Soon, the concept of interchangeable parts was introduced, and the orders the arsenal received became more and more specific in nature. As well as the mass production of uniform arms, ammunition and parts, the arsenal began several ballistics testing programs. Field tests as well as scientific lab tests were becoming more relevant to the young nation's military, making the Ordnance Department more of a priority to the generals in D.C.

Following the 1848 death of Ordnance Department commander George Bomford, who had held the position since 1812, George Talcott assumed the position of chief of ordnance. Along with his appointment came significant change and further solidification of the department's role in the American military. The War Department, whose administrators had not yet decided on a single form of primer for its small arms, soon became very interested in the scientific studies being performed at the arsenal. This fateful inquiry marked an important shift in the military's priorities, as it finally began to take seriously the science of warfare.

By 1850, the two developed methods of firearm primers were the Manyard primer, developed by American dentist Edward Manyard, and the percussion cap, which had been used by American military forces since the War of 1812. Both of these methods though, had serious faults. The Manyard primers proved too sensitive and sometimes self-ignited, and the percussion caps were too small and were often lost or misloaded. Studies at the arsenal would soon perfect the percussion cap and make it the standard for military armament.

The Ordnance Department, having gotten its wish of becoming a larger, more relevant branch, seemed oddly hesitant to adopt the new technologies being perfected at the arsenal and elsewhere. As James Farley eloquently wrote in *Making Arms in the Machine Age*, "Marked by a strong conservative streak, army officers seemed to fear rapidly firing armament—as if such weapons would engender a military promiscuity that would dilute control of battles as well as escalate the cost of warfare in both human and economic terms." As history has shown, these officers' fears were far from irrational.

As the material and scope of work being done at the arsenal became a larger priority to the Ordnance Department, arsenal commander George Ramsay developed a healthy paranoia about the property's safety. By 1850, the surrounding community of Frankford was now bustling with homes, businesses and industries, and Ramsay's concern was addressed in a letter to Talcott: "This neighborhood has become [an environment]...for lawless acts, for many months scarcely a week has elapsed without the burning of houses and barns immediately about us by organized bands of desperado." His concerns

led to the construction of a one-thousand-foot-long, seven-foot-high stone wall along the northern edge of the property, portions of which still stand today.

In 1851, George Talcott's short but sweet reign as chief of ordnance was squashed by a political revenge attack by Secretary of War Charles Conrad. Talcott was removed not only from his position in ordnance but also from the army altogether. Filling his shoes was Colonel Henry Knox Craig, a Mexican-American War hero and son of Revolutionary War officer Major Isaac Craig. Craig would prove a strong ally of the Frankford Arsenal. With his appointment as chief of ordnance, other changes were made. Major Ramsay was transferred to command the St. Louis Arsenal, and into Frankford came one of the arsenal's best, most revered administrators: Major Peter Valentine Hagner.

Hagner was a native of Washington, D.C., and had worked at Frankford previously. He had recently been working at the D.C. Arsenal, where he became very interested in—and good at—building custom machinery for the manufacture of a new form of percussion cap. His ideas would revolutionize thinking at the arsenal and bring the first pieces of physical change in four decades to its grounds. Almost immediately after being assigned as arsenal commander, Hagner began working on the percussion cap factory. Still standing today near the Tacony Street entrance, the small one-story brick building was one of the most important in the history of the arsenal.

Hagner also erected a new "French" laboratory for chemical-related explosive studies, a steam power plant and, across the empty property (and away from other buildings), a storage shed for barrels of niter. These buildings were ready for use by 1852. It seemed—whether due to the general changes in technology of the time, the further complicating web of military/political issues that affected the Ordnance Department's priorities or simply the change of administrators—that Major Hagner was

Protective steel blocks form a blast wall between two chambers inside one of the arsenal's powder magazines, where gunpowder was mixed and stored.

achieving what almost every other commander tried and failed to do: develop a trademark specialty with which to distinguish the arsenal, a purpose for its specific existence. However, he would actually achieve much more.

By 1853, the percussion cap factory—utilizing civilian child labor—was churning out more than 1 million caps monthly, and work on reshaping the caps to fit flintlock muskets was undertaken. The entire workforce of the arsenal comprised more than 1,500, including more than 200 children.

Hagner's hold on the arsenal tightened, and he received funds to erect a hospital of sufficient capacity. In 1853, the Crane Hospital was established as a place to treat the now common accident-related afflictions at the arsenal. Built far out near the property's eastern border, the hospital featured surgical rooms, a medical laboratory and two isolation wards, separate from the main hospital.

In 1854, Hagner received orders from the chief of ordnance to modify two thousand aged muskets into standard, barreled percussion lock rifles. For this task, he enlisted the help of the Remington Arms Company of Utica, New York. Working closely with arsenal machinists, Remington developed a method of conversion for the muskets from flintlock to percussion lock. This method, which required the use of a specially designed machine, was soon adopted and brought to the arsenal. Hagner had other ideas for the rifling work, however. The major himself developed a perfected prototype of a new rifling and barreling machine, which both improved the quality of the barreling cut and allowed for three barrels at once to be cut. He even attached it to steam power to allow for automatic operation.

The contract to officially produce one of Hagner's machines was finally accepted by the neighboring Bridesburg Machine Manufacturing Company. Hagner reveled at its success in 1856, stating, "My rifling machine is becoming daily more perfect in its works and more expeditious so that I can promise for it thirty barrels per day of ten hours." Most private industrial manufacturers at the time, including Bridesburg Machine, declined to produce the device. They claimed it was due to reasons such as "incapability as yet of producing heavy machinery to the degree of accuracy required" and "unsustainable cost." But Hagner knew that his machine was revolutionary. If private companies on the forefront of the Industrial Revolution failed to create what he already had, it was safe to say—with some hyperbole—that the government really *was* taking the lead in technological innovation, not free market industrialists.

It took until the end of the decade for Hagner to persuade the Ordnance Department to undertake the building, operation and maintenance of machines for the easier production and modification of arms and ammunition. By 1859, plans for a machine shop had been drawn up, and Hagner was eager to get it built. The successful installation of his cutting-edge system of arms studies and new production techniques at the arsenal inspired a large number of its employees to learn his methods and join the ranks of, as Hagner called them, his "soldier technologists." But the now escalating tensions growing between the North and South were forcing their way into every crevice of American life. As a result of the heated political feuds in

Washington over the dilemma, Secretary of War John B. Floyd removed Hagner from his post and reassigned him out to Fort Leavenworth, Kansas. Placed into his position as commander of Frankford was Josiah Gorgas, whose short term would seem like a flash in comparison to Hagner's nine years at the post.

After his removal however, Hagner's loyal group of soldier technologists, who had learned enough from him to carry on his legacy, did so with gusto. Meanwhile, as the Union army hurried to prepare for war, Gorgas—a Southerner by birth—was offered the position of chief of ordnance in the Confederate army. He quickly accepted the transfer and left the arsenal for Virginia. The frazzled Ordnance Department left the arsenal under the temporary command of Lieutenant Thomas Treadwell, who oversaw its haphazard prewar tune-up. In April 1861, Captain William Maynardier arrived as the new commander. Shortly after settling in, wartime demands reached a fever pitch. The arsenal was at its highest production rate yet, and hundreds of new civilian workers were hired. Work hours were extended, and seven-day workweeks were incorporated.

To make matters more chaotic, the Ordnance Department's funds ran out almost completely, and many arsenal workers began seeing week after week without pay. The department contractors' wages were put on hold, and even then there were insufficient finances to pay the arsenal's employees. The Treasury Department began issuing "Certificates of Indebtedness" to employees, but local businesses were not always cooperative about accepting them, and the local civilian workforce established a quick turnover rate. As the war grew more threatening, the chief of ordnance came down desperately and fiercely on the U.S. arsenals, demanding more output. Although the arsenal was operating at full capacity, Captain Maynardier was called off to Washington, and its next beloved commander— Major Theodore Thaddeus Smolenski Laidley— arrived to replace him.

Laidley was a Virginian by birth and had been a creative, bold initiate since his graduation from West Point. Laidley aggressively tackled the munitions shortage with new machines and, with them, new workers. He seemed able to drown out the pressures of wartime necessity and concentrate on building what needed to be

built in order to satisfy the Ordnance Department's demands, however impossible it seemed. Laidley always displayed confidence, stating in a letter to the chief of ordnance, "I now make only one hundred eighty [caps] per day of twenty four hours. In July I expect to make seven and a half millions, and will add a new machine every three weeks until I can make enough for the whole army."

Laidley picked up where Hagner left off with construction. Amid the frenzy of the Civil War, he focused on building. In July 1862, he received permission to build a blacksmith shop, which still stands next to Hagner's Percussion Cap Factory. Laidley intuitively introduced valuable new construction methods into the new blacksmith shop—features like reinforcement steel columns that would continue to hold the roof up in the event of an explosion, as well as the design for the columns themselves. Laidley's round support columns were made of four long, quarter-circle pieces of wrought iron bolted together at the flanked edges. This method was adopted into many other structures of the day. The new shop also included two forges and a small steam engine.

By 1863, Laidley's ideas were really coming to life. Due to several factors, including war financier Jay Cooke's uncanny fundraising abilities and Lincoln's appointment of ex-commander George D. Ramsay to the position of chief of ordnance, the new building program at the arsenal received its share of attention and financial support. At the dusk of the Civil War, the arsenal received its flagship building. The new rolling mill, completed in 1866, is truly deserving of its historic landmark status. Designed by architect John Frasier of Union League fame, the large Italianate structure was one of only a handful of nonresidential buildings built in Philadelphia during the years of the American Civil War.

Laidley's 108-foot-long, three-story rolling mill brought a strong contrast to the quaint, almost rural property. It gave the look of militarism and toughness, displaying America's new abrasive attitude toward combat, and set the design trend for the arsenal's future buildings. Laidley, however, having exhausted himself gathering materials and managing the construction of the new buildings, was dismissed as commander in 1864 due to delays in construction. Although unfairly discharged, Laidley remained one of the arsenal's most productive and intuitive commanders. His replacement was Captain Stephen Vincent Benet, who oversaw the completion of the building.

Ironically, by the time the new rolling mill opened in 1866, the nation had come almost full circle in its relationship with war. Once doing everything it could to avoid conflict, the young Union now found itself at the forefront of a new vehicle of war that, by necessity, it was forced to create. After using its ingredients for unbridled bloodshed, the war-weary republic—having longed for an end to the fighting—now resurrected a brief period of historic pacifism. Thus, the postwar years were somewhat disrespectful to the arsenal. The new buildings, after a short span of activity, saw a slowed production factor. The proud rolling mill was used for simple storage, and much of the civilian workforce was cut. Benet surely saw the work of his predecessors being taken almost for granted by a sobered Ordnance Department. It seemed that the Ordnance Department finally understood the intricacies and benefits of the Industrial Revolution.

Having begun with manual labor, the department's prerogatives—first evolving into mechanization—had now come almost 180 degrees from their origins, to complete industrialization. The concept appeared to take its time settling in with ordnance officials. While the army shyly avoided the

TOP This circa 1900 photo shows the Crane Hospital flanked by two wooden expansion wings. *Courtesy the National Library of Medicine, www.nlm.nih.gov.*

BOTTOM The Crane Hospital was built in 1853. It utilized mostly volunteer medical care, provided by local women. Sadly, it was lost to the wrecking ball in 2012.

undeniable presence of the Industrial Revolution, the Ordnance Department seemed almost afraid of adapting the sweeping new technological innovations that were beginning to wow the world. However, the soldier-technologist commanders who had taken personal virtue in furthering the cause of the arsenal had developed more than enough technological advancement there to pique the department's interest in creating what we know today as the military-industrial complex.

The years immediately following the Civil War brought the invention of the breech-loading, self-contained cartridge. This would prove to be the first chapter in America's reign in military production, and Frankford Arsenal was its focal point. These postwar years were some of the arsenal's most important. It was then that America's powerful system of industrial small-arms manufacture that we know today was born. By 1870, the arsenal's workforce saw a short rise. Defying Victorian American customs, many women found mechanical work at the arsenal very empowering. Children and young teenagers were also employed, and in some cases entire families labored together at the arsenal. The surrounding communities of Frankford and Bridesburg had also evolved industrially. Their residents no longer saw the arsenal as a loud, unwanted industrial threat to their way of life. It was, in fact, industry that connected these once very parochial neighborhoods.

In 1872, the Ordnance Department tried and failed to have a railroad line laid to the arsenal for the shipment of its goods. The city refused to allow explosives to be carried via train through residential neighborhoods. The arsenal would rely on the Delaware River as its only method of shipment until the early twentieth century. In 1876, the Ordnance Department selected the arsenal as its single facility for the production of metallic cartridges. Although repair work and other testing continued, the arsenal became solely devoted to producing these new cartridges. Laidley's testing laboratories were closed in the 1880s and used for a variety of other purposes.

Several new buildings were erected in the 1880s, including a series of ballistic-testing laboratories and storage buildings. The rolling mill was converted again, this time into a cartridge factory. With the workforce again at a low and a huge drop in contract orders, more focus was given to the grounds and buildings themselves. Gardens were planted about the property, and buildings received maintenance and cosmetic work. The eastern edge of the property, still very rural, was occupied by the arsenal's farm, barns and stables. In these peacetime decades, it was one of the most active portions of the campus. The dull monotony of life at the arsenal began to dissipate, however, when the Ordnance Department turned its interest to the study of powder chemistry.

The 1890s were the thickest years of the arsenal's relationship with the Du Pont Chemical Company of Delaware. Just prior to the Spanish-American War, great advancements were made in the field of smokeless gunpowder. The arsenal's new powder and chemical inspector, Captain John Pitman, helped perfect the new, clean-burning powder. Further testing led to a more moisture-resistant mixture, which was immediately of interest to the navy. According to author James J. Farley, by the turn of the twentieth century "the Frankford Arsenal had become the center for explosives testing in the United States." Thanks partly to the chemical advancements made there, the war was over in only a week.

The Ordnance Department received all the pep talk it needed upon the close of the war, and the testing program at the arsenal only expanded. During this postwar fervor, the arsenal received a host of ornate Spanish cannons that were captured during the war. They were infused into the façades of several buildings, set in walls beside exterior doors and windows. The new types

The Crane Hospital's surgical room still retains its decorative fireplace in this 2007 photo. The layers of paint on the original door have peeled into interesting shapes.

of small arms being introduced into the military, along with new forms of weaponry altogether—such as reciprocating, mounted antiaircraft and seacraft guns—required a completely different operational tactic. No longer could battlefield targeting be achieved with sight alone. Very specific measurements and calculations— necessary to properly aim and fire some of the new arms—required the use of special instruments. The arsenal was also in charge of designing, testing and producing these tools and sights.

America's hastened decision to enter World War I in 1917 would affect the arsenal more physically than any other single event in its history. An expansive new plan of buildings inflated the arsenal's acreage, adding another one-third of the current size to the property's northern end, beyond the old stone wall. Dozens of new buildings were erected rather quickly and were ready for use by the end of 1917. Within these buildings were mass-produced millions of artillery shells, magazines and cartridges, not to mention the powder required to fire these projectiles. Millions of other products were tested and proved, such as helmets, vehicle shields and armored cars. During the war years, the arsenal shipped out more than 100,000 shells per month and produced more than 60 million rounds of small ammunition per year.

As with many large industrial sites during the war, the arsenal filled the cuts in its civilian workforce with hundreds of women. Before "Rosie the Riveter," women at the arsenal worked in powder magazines, filling rounds with gunpowder and applying percussion caps. They also worked as welders, pressers and assemblers. By

ABOVE Considered the arsenal's architectural highlight, John Frazer's 1865 cartridge rolling mill was one of only a few structures built in Philadelphia during the Civil War.

OPPOSITE The rolling mill's shift bell was meant to signal work shifts and other events at the arsenal. It would have easily been heard from anywhere on the property. The embossed maker's mark reads, "Cast by Jos. Bernhard, 1201 s. 6 st. Philada. 1866."

1918, almost 40 percent of the arsenal's workforce of six thousand were women. No longer relying on German-made precision optical glass for gun sights, the Ordnance Department contracted the local firm of Heller and Brightly, whose employees also worked at the arsenal, to aid in the production of sight glass. Between January 1917 and November 1918, the arsenal produced 232 million rounds of ammunition—virtually every last round used by army and navy aircraft during the year. The arsenal was also the exclusive maker of incendiary and armor-piercing rounds for navy ships.

Immediately following the war, a new primer (Frankford Arsenal #70) was developed. Work began to slow, however, and the production of ammunition came to an abrupt stop. Construction of new buildings had also halted by 1922, and the arsenal resumed its role as an innovator, focused on realizing new air defense technology. Its research capabilities became more of a priority during the 1920s. By the 1930s, the spirit of science was taking charge at the arsenal, and its laboratory programs were greatly enlarged. However, the standard production of small arms and ammunition were given increasingly less attention. Although the property was enlarged for the final time, a few new structures were erected and serious advancements were achieved in the development of the Instrument Department, the peacetime decades between two world wars had softened up the arsenal's production muscles.

When the Second World War forced its way into American life, the arsenal was ill-prepared for its impact. In 1940, the Ordnance Department rather abruptly upshifted, and suddenly the weary arsenal was responsible for the manufacture of all U.S. military ammunition. By 1942, it had produced and shipped more than seventy thousand tons of product. A new itinerary was introduced for the Second World War by the War Department that helped America's industrial beasts work together to defeat the biggest enemy it had ever encountered. The Government Owned-Contractor Operated Plan (GO-CO) allowed the arsenal to instruct representatives from other government-contracted manufacturers—such as Bendix, Eastman-Kodak, Westinghouse and Winchester—to produce and gauge its designs. Given blueprints, gauges, special instruments and calculations, these representatives returned to their companies, which were quickly outproducing the opposition.

When the biggest conflict in history was finally over, the arsenal found itself without its minerals. Having given away all of its innovations to win the war, the campus of more than two hundred buildings emerged somehow less coveted. It continued to do its duty of producing and researching, but the unique heroics that had made the Frankford Arsenal the grandfather of the American military-industrial complex were just memories. Brief revivals in production for the Korean War and Vietnam were the last spikes of life for the century-and-a-half-old arsenal. Its workforce thinned out, its equipment and facilities were transferred or removed and, by the bicentennial year of 1976, the Defense Department had announced the arsenal's official closure. In 1978, after several ideas for the property's relocation or reuse, it was given to the city by the federal government.

In 1981, the current owner, Hankin Properties, purchased the arsenal. It became the Arsenal Business Center, housing private and commercial lessees. The eastern end of the property has been sold off; part of it is a public riverside park area with boat access. The majority of the eastern half now belongs to the Dietz and Watson Company. After three decades of use as a business park, half of the remaining campus was demolished in 2012, with plans to erect a shopping center on the site. Today, the arsenal houses the Special Victims Unit of the Philadelphia Police

The design and placement of the rolling mill's main stairwell is a good example of the bold yet restrained look of Philadelphia's Victorian military architecture.

Department, the Franklin Town Charter School, the Philadelphia Rare Books and Manuscripts Company and several other businesses. Several of its structures, such as the rolling mill and percussion cap factory, as well as the original parade grounds and surrounding buildings, are listed on the National Register of Historic Places and await reuse. With most of its remaining buildings currently vacant, it looks hopeful that the arsenal's rich history will be enjoyed by future generations through the continued preservation efforts of its owner.

Philadelphia Naval Shipyard

Although constructed in the early 1940s, the soldiers' barracks at the navy yard appears far more aged. Its dormitories hosted thousands of enlisted men until the 1990s.

PHILADELPHIA IS TRULY LUCKY to have had the presence of its naval shipyard on League Island. The former swampland at the extreme southern tip of Philadelphia was considered an unimportant, unwanted appendage of the city. Running one league in length from east to west, League Island has proven itself one of America's most important landmasses. The League Island Navy Yard was the only freshwater naval facility in the country, and it was once geographically the largest naval shipbuilder in the world. By the mid-eighteenth century, at least three of the thirteen original colonies had already constructed forts and warships for their own defense.

Philadelphia's was the largest port in the colonies. Its many shipbuilders churned out dozens of wooden ships before the revolution. Although Philadelphia was the largest and most populated city in the colonies, the Quaker government, ironically, strictly forbade any construction relating to its own defense, let alone military action.

Despite the founder's ideals, Philadelphians were divided on the issue. Some were strongly opposed to the idea of building ships for anything other than trade purposes. Others were determined to establish a line of defense in the quickly escalating conflict with France. The sheepish proprietors learned a bitter lesson,

An empty bunk room in the soldiers' barracks. Once stacked with bunk beds and alive with the sound of military slang, the barracks today house only pigeons.

The burly reinforced concrete seaplane hangar at Mustin Naval Airfield was erected at the start of World War II and was later used as a department store for resident yard workers. Recently, it has been used as a film set for movies like *Law Abiding Citizen*, *Transformers: Revenge of the Fallen* and *The Last Airbender*.

however, and Quaker pacifism began to give way to fearful necessity during the French and Indian War. Philadelphia's first navy yard was thus unofficially established in an area then known as Wicaco, just below Old Swedes Church (current intersection of Columbus Boulevard and Washington Avenue). There, at the ship works of James and

Thomas Penrose, Pennsylvania's first warship, *Hero*, was built in 1762. After the successful launch of *Hero*, the shipbuilders of Wicaco petitioned to the provincial legislature to rename the area Southwark, after London's shipbuilding district.

When James Penrose died in 1771, his young apprentice, Joshua Humphreys Jr., took over the business

and soon completed the three-hundred-ton ship *Sally*. He partnered with John Wharton and extended their river frontage. Just as Philadelphia was on the verge of war with Great Britain and new ships would have seemed necessary, work at the navy yard halted. As the Tories and Revolutionaries fought with each other over the course of action the legislature should take, the situation was getting worse. Finally, on June 30, 1775, a bill was passed to raise a militia and fortify the city. Left in the hands of a Committee of Safety headed by Benjamin Franklin and Robert Morris, a group of "minutemen" was raised, and work began on Fort Mifflin.

Franklin's committee was also given the authority to dispense military contracts to local shipyards for warships. Enlisting the out-of-work shipwrights of Kensington and Southwark, contracts were given to several shipyards along the Delaware, including the Penrose shipyard.

The lobby area of the former Mustin Naval Airfield administration building shows how badly the structure has been water damaged. It was last used in the mid-1990s as a career transition office for longtime League Island employees.

After only months of construction, the contracted yards produced thirteen armed ships, and Franklin handed over to the Pennsylvania Assembly his calculated costs. But most thought the ships far too weak to withstand a British attack and scolded Franklin for his underwhelming efforts. The great American genius, however, was not interested in matters of defense, for he had far more pressing obligations as a member of the Committee of Secret Correspondence and the Continental Congress.

The burden of local defense and experimental arms had fallen to Franklin's partner, Robert Morris. Morris acted promptly and laid out plans for what would become the first U.S. naval shore facility. Basically a geographical merger of the aforementioned existing Southwark shipyards, Morris's conglomeration extended more than a quarter mile along the Delaware. It contained several shipyards, a recruiting office, a supply warehouse, a paymaster's office and an office for a new naval planning board. A new

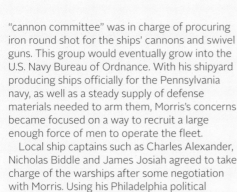

"cannon committee" was in charge of procuring iron round shot for the ships' cannons and swivel guns. This group would eventually grow into the U.S. Navy Bureau of Ordnance. With his shipyard producing ships officially for the Pennsylvania navy, as well as a steady supply of defense materials needed to arm them, Morris's concerns became focused on a way to recruit a large enough force of men to operate the fleet.

Local ship captains such as Charles Alexander, Nicholas Biddle and James Josiah agreed to take charge of the warships after some negotiation with Morris. Using his Philadelphia political connections, Morris established a system of recruitment from local militia leaders. A pleasing turnout of dozens willing to serve as "Minute Men on Board the Boats when required" eased Morris's mind, if only briefly. During the long, hot summer of 1775, the Continental Congress painfully debated over whether or not to establish a national navy. Many were opposed to the idea, citing financial constraints. Maryland delegate Samuel Chase voiced his opinion rather bluntly: "It is the maddest idea in the world to think of building an American fleet, as we would mortgage the whole continent."

The debate roared on throughout the summer, and Congress finally agreed to fund the construction of two armed warships. But by October, British ships had become a more frequent sight along the coast, and Congress began to feel the squeeze. It approved a new naval committee, which included John Adams and Richard Henry Lee of Virginia, but did not include a Pennsylvania representative. After the new committee tried and failed several times to obtain four armed warships, it finally turned to the official president of the Pennsylvania Defense Committee, Benjamin Franklin. Perhaps as a shy rebuttal for not being included in the Continental naval committee, Franklin's maneuvering sealed the fate of the new Continental navy, as well as its role in Philadelphia's history. His ingenious agreement with Pennsylvania's rowdy privateers created legal pirates who were willing to fight the British.

Robert Morris's still new Pennsylvania naval shipyard embraced its important role as one of the first shipyards to officially produce watercraft for the U.S. Navy. The old Pennsylvania Defense Committee had no trouble acquiring the navy's first nine ships, two of which were purchased from old Philadelphia merchants. Originally built by the old Pennsylvania Defense Committee, the four-hundred-ton brig *Black Prince* was acquired and renamed *Alfred* by its new commander, Philadelphia ship master John Barry. The ship received a thorough overhaul and reinforcement and was equipped with twenty nine-pound and ten six-pound cannons.

Congress next acquired the aforementioned Penrose and Wharton ship *Sally*, which was renamed *Columbus* and received twenty-eight guns. In November 1775, the 112-ton brig *Defiance* was obtained, strengthened, fitted with sixteen cannons and renamed *Andrea Doria*. In December, the nation's first fleet of warships was ready for sail down the icy Delaware. Meanwhile, the leading force behind the organization of the new fleet, Robert Morris, was pushing the importance of his position with the new Congress and asking for a salary. He was elected a Pennsylvania congressman and then became chairman of Congress's Secret Committee of Commerce. Morris used his clout with Congress to put more attention (and money) into its naval interests. This ensured that Philadelphia's shipbuilding community of Southwark would only strengthen its reign on the Continental navy.

However, differences with Congress over how best to protect Morris's precious fleet on the Delaware from an inevitable British attack ate away at their relationship. When Washington's famous surprise attacks at Trenton and Princeton in late 1776 caused the British to focus more efforts there, it was thought that the ships, and possibly even Philadelphia, were safe from an attack. Unfortunately, by 1777, British forces had taken the city. During their occupation, some of Southwark's shipbuilders—fearing execution or imprisonment—continued to work on their ships, but for the British navy. Ironically, after British forces departed Philadelphia in 1778, they were all hanged for treason by the Continental Congress.

After the conflict had ended, and Philadelphia had hosted the Constitutional Convention, Treasury Secretary Alexander Hamilton's plan for the regional dispersal of the new nation's vital ingredients designated the Mid-Atlantic as its center of "dockyards and arsenals." But contracts for naval ships went out to shipbuilders up and down the coast, from Massachusetts to Georgia. It was clear that the old Southwark shipyards had lost their hold on the nation's naval interests. They did continue business as usual, however, and launched the *General Greene* in 1792. President Washington raised the production of ships after the Philadelphia-built *President*, along with ten other ships, were captured by the Barbary State of Algiers.

The Philadelphia Naval Shipyard operated at an up-and-down pace over the course of the next half century. In 1861, its eager new commander, Captain Samuel F. Du Pont, prepared the yard for the great country's war with itself. But the impact was not what he was expecting. Du Pont, of the wealthy Delaware family, frantically juggled the constant, unwanted technicalities that came with the oncoming conflict. The endless supply of damaged ships that flowed into the shipyard for repair proved too much for it to handle by the end of the war. The area surrounding the Southwark shipyard was approaching its full industrial horsepower, as factories and businesses squeezed the tiny property in, making access exceedingly more difficult.

What became abundantly clear was that the region needed a new government naval facility. This meant that Philadelphia would once again have to fight for itself against other states that recognized the financial and political gain that came with hosting a navy yard. City officials immediately offered up its unwanted appendage—League Island—to the government for use as a new navy yard. However, Congress did not seem in favor of a site in crowded Philadelphia and eyed more closely locations in New London, Connecticut, and Narragansett Bay, Rhode Island. Throughout the Civil War, Philadelphia urged Congress to take possession of the swampy nest of mosquitoes at its southern tip, but the political process dragged on.

By the war's end in 1865, the Navy Department had a dozen warships ready for repair docked along the muddy edge of League Island, but Congress had still not officially accepted the site. After finally agreeing to visit the site personally

and seeing what had turned into several dozen ships and ironclads already docked, the assistant secretary of the navy agreed to accept Philadelphia's offer. But further political fighting shredded the idea. It was not until 1874 that a serious decision to occupy League Island as a naval shipyard was at last reached, and it was not until 1876 that the Navy Department officially named it as government property.

Before its fill of dredged earth from the former Smith's and Burlington Islands, the eastern half of League Island had been nothing but swampy, buggy marshlands. After the fill, its man-made flatland was almost useless. But when aviation took the country by storm in the first decade of the twentieth century, League Island's endless open land became immediately recognized as a perfect flying field. As early as 1910, the Aero Club of Pennsylvania laid a runway and built a small hangar there. Soon after, the navy built a receiving station, temporary barracks and a hospital, all for quarantined sailors who returned with influenza and other contagious diseases.

The First World War changed everything on the island. American armed forces, although advanced in tactical combat, still clung to the basic principals of seventeenth- and eighteenth-century warfare. Forming lines and advancing into volleys of rounds was finally starting to be seen as perhaps not the best method of military action. New strategies combined with new technologies led to new attitudes about war, as well as new fears. With the largest and most experienced armies on earth doing battle with one another for control of Europe, World War I was not surprisingly seen as the "war to end all wars." And in 1917, when the fighting finally forced a very disinterested America to join the Allied forces, no form of military technology was overlooked. The new concept of flying machines was definitely one that piqued the military's interest.

Every aviation company and manufacturer of airplanes and nautical parts in the country was put to use building bombers and transport planes for the army. The navy, too, pressed the importance of its need for aircraft and put in orders for a small number of planes. It was decided, however, that the tiny number of aircraft requested by the navy would take a backseat to the army's much larger orders, and contracts for the private manufacture of seaplanes for the navy were cancelled. As a result, naval officials began developing means for the navy to erect its own aircraft. Headed by the efforts of aviation captain Henry Croskey Mustin and Marine Corps aviator Alfred A. Cunningham, eastern League Island became Philadelphia's first official naval aircraft facility. The navy's new venture of building small seaplanes and flying boats finally took shape on July 27, 1917, with the opening of the Mustin Naval Air Facility, named for the most adamant champion of its cause.

Mustin's impressive plea to navy officials must have done the trick, as the new airfield was granted more than $2 million for construction. The navy, grudgingly, would have to share League Island with the new airfield. However, logistics quickly forced its cooperation. Several buildings were erected by 1918, including a new hangar, a seven-story aircraft production factory, two single-story barracks, an administration building, a radio communication tower and several other structures. Soon after these buildings opened, the island's need for more power became apparent. The power plant on the west side of the island was not sufficient for the existing navy yard buildings as well as the new ones. The Philadelphia Electric Company was called on to build a new power plant, which sits just south of the former Mustin Airfield administration building (naval headquarters). The small, Windrim and Elgin–designed generating plant contained two Westinghouse Turbines and was just over capacity.

The First World War also kept the field of naval weaponry on the front burner of American military priorities. New advancements in ammunition and powder manufacture at Frankford Arsenal brought on more weapon-based programs at the Navy Yard. New moisture-resistant powder was tested, and locally manufactured mounted guns were installed and tested aboard hundreds of ships. More than eleven thousand workers pushed the yard's output to record numbers. It does not seem odd then, that the armistice of 1918 was a sobering slap for employees, shaking them out of their monotonously weary routines. For a brief period, the yard's output slowed almost to a stop. But by 1919, it had sprung up fast, surpassing even wartime production.

By 1920, the necessity of Mustin Field was proving undeniable. More funds were granted for the erection of a testing laboratory where more aspects of flight could be studied. As the aircraft factory enlarged, the testing facility took on bigger and bolder experimental projects. Naval projects were worked on as well, such as the conversion of old coal-powered engine systems to more efficient oil-burning systems. League Island was in its best dress for the city's sesquicentennial celebration in 1926. The swamplands just to its north were filled in and beautified for use as the main grounds of the exhibition. Residential development quickly followed, and League Island was no longer separated from mainland Philadelphia. The southwestern portion of the sesqui grounds still exists today as Franklin Delano Roosevelt Park.

After the first blows of the Great Depression, the navy yard received its biggest boost yet under Roosevelt's New Deal. In 1934, the Vinson-Trammell Naval Construction Act poured funding and purpose into the yard. By 1938, it had produced more than fifteen new ships. But by that time it was also realized that the yard's pace was far too slow to even make a dent in the looming German and Japanese forces. In 1939, after the invasion of Poland, the navy yard assumed full mobilization. By November, workers at the yard had recommissioned forty-five Destroyers. President Roosevelt's tour of League Island in 1940 impressed the busy man, who promised the city $4 million to expand the yard. He also

The immense roof of building 624 appears at first glance to be a ground-level landscape, although it is, in fact, nine tall stories above the ground. Although the largest remaining structure on League Island, the building was constructed in just several months for the Second World War.

added eleven thousand new jobs at the yard and erected the Penrose Housing Project for yard workers.

A new dry dock was added in 1941, and on it was built the forty-five-thousand-ton battleship *Wisconsin*. After the attack on Pearl Harbor, the yard issued blackout policies, where all lights were turned off at night to deter bombing raids. The Mustin Naval Aircraft Facility employed more than 25 percent of the total workforce, and once again, women filled thousands of positions throughout League Island. A proposition by navy commanders to use German prisoners of war for labor at the navy yard was very seriously considered before being refused. League Island also experienced tension when thousands of "nonwhite" employees were allowed to work at the yard during the war. Many of its workers picketed, went on strike and sometimes used violence to express their disapproval of the new interracial, unisex policies.

By 1943, the civilian workforce on League Island had swelled to 58,434, its peak. The daily commutes of this many people to and from the yard created new problems. Soon work was underway on several barracks, which sprang up with amazing speed. The barracks were expanded several times before the end of the war. The architectural firm Zanzinger and Borie intuitively designed and quickly built the General Storehouse (building 624) in 1942. Its simple construction method allowed for easy expansion. A year later, it was doubled in size, nearly reaching an impressive 500,000 square feet. More than two dozen new structures had been added by the end of 1944.

At the close of the war, thousands of men and women, civilian and personnel, were employed at the yard. Although its workforce shrunk significantly after the war, more than one thousand still lived on site. Postwar sociological advancements pushed the old military style of housing its workers in large barracks out of popular consensus. New row homes were built after the war on a portion of Mustin Field. Ordinary row homes, identical to those simultaneously filling up the northeast, provided a real sense of home life for PNSY workers. By 1960, more than one thousand employees and their families were living on the site, and public relations efforts strengthened the yard's relationship with Philadelphia.

The Cold War played tricks on League Island. Although no fighting took place, national politics was not on the side of large industrial naval shipyards. Financial, social and technological changes in Washington, D.C., were foreboding to employees and advocates of the Philadelphia Naval Shipyard. They saw a threat to their lives' work, and when some in the Kennedy administration advised the closure of several large naval facilities throughout the United States, including League Island, serious fears abounded in Philadelphia. However, when Kennedy himself decided against closing League Island, employees were relieved. But at the beginning of the Johnson administration, PSNY was back in the red. Johnson, too, had a strong desire to reduce funding for large naval facilities, but he was at the beginning of his term and worked the issue at a slow pace.

After property assessments by federal agencies and endless graph and chart presentations, the decision was finally made to keep League Island open. In the end, it was the yard's herculean size and muscle that saved it. Defense Secretary Robert McNamara explained that the yard was twice the size, contained the best facilities and had the most industrially advantageous physical layout of any naval yard on the East Coast. When President Johnson increased defense spending in 1964, League Island received a physical facelift of new buildings and the refurbishment of its existing structures.

During the 1960s, the navy introduced its Service Life Extension

This view shows a stairwell in the soldiers' barracks. Its caged-off floor access relays the strict nature of military service. The building's echoey halls now only reflect the sound of silence.

In the 1970s, the Mustin Homes were constructed to house navy yard workers and their families. Here, shortly before demolition in 2013, the housing units sit in silence, eerily resembling a post-apocalyptic scene.

Attached to the roof of the former Aircraft Storage Building facing the former site of the Municipal Stadium, the words "Go Navy" once lit up the night during the annual Army/Navy football games.

Program (SLEP) at League Island. Some of the yard's resources went to repairing and refitting old ships, while still holding contracts for the building of new ones. League Island was the perfect location for this new endeavor. Its freshwater dry docks offered the ability to completely disassemble large ships, a process that often took years, without the worry of saltwater corrosion. By 1966, SLEP was at its peak. League Island employed more than thirteen thousand civilian workers and more than two thousand enlisted personnel. In 1968, the yard received the contract to refurbish the sixty-thousand-ton aircraft carrier *Saratoga*,

which was the largest ship to ever grace League Island. Amazingly, the entire vessel was overhauled in just under one year.

After the yard turned out a shiny, refurbished USS *New Jersey*, word began to circulate hinting at the navy's decision to subcontract all new work out to private shipyards. This was a devastating concept to most on League Island. The rumors soon became fact, and in 1968, naval officials announced that League Island would direct all its future efforts to SLEP. In 1969, the last naval ship to be built on League Island, the USS *Blue Ridge*, was launched. Although the navy's budget was on a steady decline due to popular antiwar sentiment, the business of overhauling old ships saw a brief but profitable rise in 1971, when the yard still accommodated more than twelve thousand civilian workers and more than three thousand enlisted personnel.

Enlisted men and their families lived in a new residential community laid out over much of the unused Mustin Field. It featured a recreation center, a movie theater, a swim club, three schools (including a facility for special needs children), a post office, restaurants (including a McDonald's) and several recreation areas, such as Coronado Park at the northeast extremity of the island. Coronado Park was reminiscent of any state park. Its gazebos, barbecue pavilions and shooting range were often used by the Boy Scouts. The enormous seaplane hangar was converted into a department store and commissary. A fully integrated bus route was also in place across the yard, with bus shelters set up every eighth of a mile.

As the work-hungry yard received bigger contracts for ship overhaul, its reputation soon made it known as the largest refurbisher of naval vessels in the United States. More worker housing was necessary. Fortunately, land was plentiful at the former Mustin Airfield. Enlisting the help of the Philadelphia Industrial Development Corporation (PIDC), the navy expanded the residential community for League Island employees. At the extreme eastern quadrant of the island, Mustin Homes was erected in the 1970s as a modern, home-like housing development, complete with playgrounds, easy parking and affordable costs. Beginning in the 1980s, five aircraft carriers were overhauled at the yard at a cost of more than $3 billion.

Mustin Homes residents began leaving in the early 1990s, however, as talk of closure loomed. The prefab community was completely empty by 1996. Although other ideas for its use were thrown back and forth, the little neighborhood on League Island never again saw tenancy. During the years of its abandonment, however, the Navy Seals used the environment for training. Its safe distance from civilization allowed them to train "hot" (using live ammunition) and have their

way with the flimsy housing units. Aside from the Seals' occasional visits, the detached Mustin Homes barely saw humans. In fact, its desolate state attracted rare wildlife, such as bald eagles and hawks.

The official closure of the yard finally came in 1994, followed by a year of indecision. The Clinton administration, working closely with Governor Ed Rendell, reached an easy decision to lease parts of the property to private businesses, redevelop other parts and sell off the rest. The majority of the property became the Philadelphia Naval Business Center, offering accessible, strong, historically significant buildings that could be easily converted to house just about any type of business the yard hoped to accommodate. The western third of the island was sold to a European shipbuilding company that still owns it today.

In 2004, the Norfolk Southern Company leased the airfield for use as the Mustin Intermodal Facility—a transfer point for goods being shipped, from rail to air or vice versa. Problems with union contracts forced the operation to close, however, a short time later. By 2006, the entire eastern half of League Island was as desolate as a desert, and its collection of wildlife grew. Still a vital wetland, the area is important to the city's water table, as it helps prevent flooding. The presence of the rotting Mustin Homes, in the middle of the most barren area in Philadelphia, was truly a rare and interesting sight. The modern community, physically identical to any in the northeast, in its abandoned state was the closest thing to a post-apocalyptic scene one could ask for.

It is almost unfortunate, then, that the homes were demolished in 2013. Today, most of what remains inhabited of League Island is undergoing a thorough rehabilitation. The grounds have been beautifully landscaped into a parklike setting, with benches and scenic views along the yard's southern river frontage. Local industries like the Tasty Baking Company, as well as international corporations, currently operate facilities at the Naval Business Center. For the sake of history, hopefully the future of League Island is as long and industrious as its past.

CHAPTER 6

RESIDENTIAL

They say home is where the heart is, and Philadelphia has been called the "city of homes." A place to build a life has been probably the most iconic piece of the American dream. A small piece of land that included a modest home in an English manor–style yard was the norm for the first land purchasers of Pennsylvania. However, even those who could not afford to buy or build a home for themselves had opportunities in Philadelphia. The English nobility system did not reach into the New World until the early eighteenth century, and many new landowners rented and leased portions of their land to other eager colonists. The new American city offered a standard of living that was simply not available to many in Europe. A home, including land for farming, and a tax-based system of securities was promised to all land purchasers. Most new colonists settled along the busy waterfront area of the old city. Some lived in caves along the riverside until Penn's charter of laws removed them. But the majority of new settlers had means to erect row homes along the city's new streets.

Still, from the beginning, there were those with wealth and greater means of survival. Some built large mansions in the congested Old City area, and others spread farther north, south and west and erected massive estates on vast stretches of open land. The wealthy families of the nineteenth century spread out even farther. Neighborhoods that are still today occupied by the upper class like Elkins Park, Chestnut Hill and Mount Airy have not changed as much in two hundred years. Other areas, such as Hartranft, Wynnefield, Strawberry Mansion and Northern Liberties, although today very urban neighborhoods, were once home to some of the city's richest Gilded Age entrepreneurs. Today, the quality of Philadelphia's homes is still one of the city's finest features. Although many neighborhoods' ethnic identities have changed, Philadelphia retains its title as a city of homes. This chapter will showcase two such multigenerational estates whose remnants have refused to rot away.

Parkgate-McIlhenny Residence

ALTHOUGH PRIMARILY a city of middle-class Americans, Philadelphia was also a launching pad for many intuitive inventors. In the decades after the Civil War, a determined Irish immigrant named John McIlhenny perfected the first mechanical natural gas meter. Quickly patenting his invention, McIlhenny formed his business in 1879 with partner William Helme. The family's middle-class home near Germantown became larger and larger as McIlhenny's fortune grew. The family's endless love of fine art, in America at least, started with John. His son, John Dexter McIlhenny, joined his father's business at a young age and became heavily involved with the company's contracts. Upon the elder John's retirement around the turn of the twentieth century, John D. became president of the company. Taking the family's love of art a step further, he pressed politically and financially for a new art museum for the city.

It wasn't long before John D. McIlhenny was amassing a fortune of his own. In 1898, he married fellow art connoisseur Frances Galbraith Plumer, a daughter of Philadelphia money. In 1908, John D. hired the architectural firm of Duhring, Okie & Zeigler to design a new mansion for him and his planned family in the flourishing Pelham section. John D. and Frances had four children: John Dexter Jr., Frances (who died soon after her birth), Bernice and Henry. The picturesque American family seems almost as perfect as the art they collected. In 1909, the McIlhennys moved into their new mansion fronting Lincoln Drive, which was situated along the overlapping edges of Pelham, Mount Airy and Germantown, near the current intersection of Wayne and Johnson Streets.

Made completely of Wissahickon schist, the Colonial Revival–style house was fireproof. The detached carriage house and garage was also made from the rare gray stone. A sloping, rocky hill separated the towering house from the Wissahickon Creek and Lincoln Drive. Views from even its first-floor parlor windows provided a scene that is today uncapturable, one that not just an art collector could appreciate. The house's location, at one end of the recently developed Fairmount Park, was surely the inspiration for its name, Parkgate. As did his father, John D. relied heavily on the success of the United Gas Improvement Company (UGI), without which the sales of his gas meters would surely plummet.

In 1916, the founder of the family fortune, John McIlhenny Sr., died at the age of eighty-six. His art collection, worth almost $200,000 at the time, was passed to John D., along with the company. As a result, John D. again hired the same architectural firm to enlarge Parkgate with a gallery for his father's collection, among other additions. Now a full house, Parkgate must have been one expensive playground for John D.'s youngest child, Henry. Born in 1910, Henry was coveted by his mother and seemingly inherited an even bigger obsession with the fine arts. His education in Boston only exposed him to more of the arts, feeding his interest. At the age of fifteen, Henry's collection began with two bronze statues that he purchased while vacationing in Egypt.

Dense woods have surrounded John D. McIlhenny's Parkgate. Remnants of its use as part of Lingelbach Elementary School linger in the form of rusty playground equipment.

While simultaneously battling the Philadelphia Electric Company (PECO)—UGI's archrival—both in the courts and on the market, John D. continued his allegiance to the gas trust. In 1918, he began his tenure as the president of the slowly developing Philadelphia Museum of Art. His passion for sharing his art collection with the world was clearly his driving force. He donated his own art and money against the will of the Vare political machine, whose corruption had held up the construction process for almost two decades. During the graft-filled '20s, while the new art museum was being erected, John D. saw to it that the museum's collection was as pristine as could be in its temporary location at Memorial Hall in Fairmount Park. He gave much of his father's collection to

the museum, as well as pieces from his own. All the while, he instilled the importance of philanthropy and charity at the museum, and Henry must have been listening.

At the threshold of a real art museum, John D. met future curator Fiske Kimball. The two worked together and acquired more funding and collections. John D. appointed Kimball as museum curator and trusted him with the most pressing financial issues of the museum. While McIlhenny and Kimball worked well together, they apparently did not like each other much. Their differences were overlooked, however, for the good of the museum both men cared desperately about. After his years of tireless efforts, big spending, lawsuits and political dancing, John D. McIlhenny died in 1925, never seeing his beloved museum come to fruition. His reputation as an art lover and founding father of the Philadelphia Museum of Art still holds strong today. Henry unwittingly followed in his father's footsteps. He was now the man of the house and the beneficiary of most of his father's art collection, which by now was worth close to $1 million. He lived at Parkgate until 1929, when he headed off to Boston to attend Harvard.

At the insistence of his mother, who joined the museum staff in 1925 and served on the Associate Committee of Women, Henry studied the fine arts under Paul Sachs, who was one of New England's biggest collectors. While at Harvard, Henry took a liking to the eighteenth-century French painting *Still Life with a Hare*. His mother purchased the painting for Henry, further fueling his interest in French art. Soon, Henry began officially building his own collection. He acquired pieces by Toulouse-Lautrec, Matisse, Renoir and others. Henry graduated from Harvard in 1933 as a member of Phi Beta Kappa. Fiske Kimball became the museum director after John D.'s death and offered Henry a position on the staff upon his graduation. Later that year, Henry joined the ranks of the museum and became assistant curator of decorative arts. He referred to Kimball as a "Germanic boor" and often joked that Kimball was the reason for his father's death.

When his older brother, John Dexter Jr., died in 1935, Henry's relationship with his last remaining sibling, his older sister, Bernice, grew stronger. Henry took to the museum like it was second nature. At least three generations of serious love for the arts showed in his uncanny ability to acquire new collections, and Henry was promoted to curator of decorative arts in 1939. He surpassed his job title from the start and began organizing shows and local art clubs as early as 1936. It is not surprising, given Henry's experience and knowledge of the arts, that his new organizations and exhibitions were extremely well received. He began developing his flawless reputation as an art collector and connoisseur with the success of these exhibitions. He also brought Bernice on board the museum staff and involved her in the planning of exhibits.

When the Second World War rocked America, Henry enlisted in the Naval Reserve in 1942. He became a lieutenant in the Aviation Volunteer Special Class, serving twenty-nine months. Almost half his time at war was spent aboard the USS *Bunker Hill*, which saw action in the Pacific. During the war, Henry's mother died, and Bernice arranged the burial. Upon his return home in 1946, Henry spent a year at Parkgate. He then took a leave of absence from the museum in 1947 to spend a year in Italy, where he fell in love with Italian Renaissance art and was reportedly frustrated that he could not "buy it all." When he returned home again to Parkgate, Henry dealt with a bit of a midlife crisis. However, matured and refocused, he purchased the exquisite 1858 four-story mansion in Rittenhouse Square—Philadelphia's richest area—in 1950. At Parkgate, Henry hosted very exclusive parties featuring some of the wealthiest and most influential art collectors in the world. They were somewhat of a last hurrah for his childhood home.

By the time he moved into his Rittenhouse Square home, his parties had become renowned among elite New York and Philadelphia art circles. He moved into the house, along with his remaining art collection, in 1952. Soon, Henry bought the two neighboring mansions to enlarge his own. He also built an art gallery and courtyard on the adjacent property and adored entertaining high-profile guests and throwing lavish parties there, showing off his collection. He openly displayed his art to visitors, saying that it seemed "more sympathetic in a private home." Queens, princes, actors, artists and politicians passed through Henry's home, and he was not shy about having them. In fact, he was hailed by Andy Warhol—a frequent guest at his parties—as "the only man in Philadelphia with glamour."

After bidding a fond farewell to his childhood home, Henry went to Ireland for a time, where he purchased a nine-hundred-year-old castle, Glenveagh. Although Parkgate was appraised for $160,000 in 1951, Henry donated the mansion and its grounds to the School District of Philadelphia in 1954. One year later, the Lingelbach Elementary School was erected on a section of the property. The carriage house and garage were demolished for an athletic yard, and the house was used by the school as an annex. The elegantly manicured grounds were paved over for a parking lot, and children's play equipment was installed around the house. While Parkgate was awkwardly being surrounded by the bustling public school, its presence

quickly became hidden from future generations. Sandwiched between thick woods and a large modern school, the mansion was used only by students and teachers throughout the 1960s and '70s.

It was not until the 1980s that Parkgate became relevant again. The discovery of asbestos throughout the building led to its immediate closure, and it was sealed tight. The playground equipment surrounding the house continued to be used by schoolchildren for several years until it was deemed too dangerous due to asbestos exposure. As a result, the current state of overgrowth around the building began its strangling of Parkgate. Henry McIlhenny died in 1986, leaving behind one of the largest art collections ever owned by a Philadelphian. Upon his death, Henry donated the entire collection to the museum. The value of his art collection alone was estimated at more than $100 million. Henry was buried in his family's plot at West Laurel Hill Cemetery in Bala Cynwyd.

Today, Parkgate is largely ignored, unknown to many even in the surrounding neighborhood. Its original sculpture gardens are all but gone, and the small portion that is left is buried under a sea of rampant ivy. The house itself still looms in the dark, woodsy corner of the Lingelbach Elementary School property. Its north façade, with its boarded windows and doors, acts as a backdrop for the school's basketball courts, which are frequently occupied by neighborhood youth. The accent trees along the mansion's south façade have gone decades without a trimming and are beginning to damage the roof. The playground equipment sits rusting and wrapped in nature. The only occupants of the home's interior are a family of raccoons and the occasional homeless squatter. A guard vulture keeps watch over the house from his nest on the roof. Recent interest in the house has led to more substantial discussions about its preservation. However, nothing has yet proved fruitful, and Parkgate remains another forgotten connection to one of Philadelphia's many prized personalities.

Heidelberg's enormous historic presence is metaphorically captured in this 2010 photograph. The towering tree in the center is more than two centuries old.

Heidelberg/Kerlin Farm

JUST OUTSIDE THE CITY LIMITS, in the town of Cheltenham, sat one of the most historic structures in the entire region until recently. Sadly, its past did not warrant enough interest in its preservation. One of Philadelphia's northwestern borders, Cheltenham Avenue separates the city from the borough of Cheltenham, in Montgomery County. Cheltenham was settled by several of William Penn's original land purchasers. Among them was a Quaker by the name of Everard Bolton. Bolton's original one-hundred-acre purchase was one of the first in Cheltenham, and he is regarded as one of its founding fathers. The Bolton name is one of long heritage in England, going back more than six hundred years.

Bolton arrived in Philadelphia aboard the ship *Bristol Factor* in 1682, along with his wife and two children. In 1694, he bought four hundred more acres of land in Cheltenham from another one of Penn's original purchasers, William Brown. Bolton's total acreage then made up about one-third of what is today the borough of Cheltenham. Soon after this purchase, Bolton erected a small single-story fieldstone house near the present-day intersection of Oak Lane and Ashbourne Roads. The quaint little square house was typical of Quaker farmhouses of the day—extremely utilitarian, with no decoration or design. The house was twenty-five by twenty-seven feet and rose about seventeen feet above the ground. This original structure would become the "center block" of a much larger structure.

Everard's involvement with the local Abington Friends Meeting grew as he more strongly credited his religious faith for his fruitful new life. He earned his title, however, as a founding father of the area, being one of the co-creators and founders of the Abington Friends School. The eager young pacifist helped organize the Byberry and Langhorne Friends Meetings. He also became involved in local politics, serving on the Pennsylvania Assembly. Everard and his wife had eleven children by the time of her death in 1707, nine of whom survived. Everard soon remarried to Margaret Waterman Jones, the recently widowed wife of Philadelphia businessman John Jones. In 1712, Everard retired to Southampton Township to focus on his true love: spirituality. He signed the deed to his Cheltenham property over to his son Everard Jr.:

To all to whom these Presents shall Come, Everard Bolton Senr. of the Township of Southampton in the County of Bucks and Province of Pennsylvania, Yeoman Sends Greetings, Know Ye' that Everard Bolton as well for the Natural Love and Affection that I have for my Eldest son Everard Boltoun. Me at this time moving have Given and Granted and by these Presents do fully clearly and absolutely give Grant and Confirm unto him the said Everard Boltoun a certain Tract or Parcel of Land Situate and being in the Cheltnham Township…With all the Houses Orchards Gardens Fields Woods Underwoods Water Courses Ways Wasts Commons Mines Minerals Fishings Fowlings Huntings.

Everard Jr.'s time at the homestead was cut short, however, in 1715, when he contracted a disease (probably smallpox) and died at thirty-six years old. Being the sole landowner, he penned a will on his deathbed, leaving everything to his six-year-old son, Samuel:

> *I, Everard Bolton, of Cheltenham Township, County of Philadelphia* [Montgomery], *Province of Pennsylvania, being very sick and weak in body but of sound and perfect memory, will and bequeath to my son Samuel if he attains to the age of twenty one years all my said plantation with all ye buildings.*

When Everard Sr. died in 1727, his will gave all his remaining properties to his sons and widow. He can rest contently, however, for his bloodline carried on into some of the most interesting relations one could hope to have in colonial America. His grandson married Betsy Ross's older sister, Deborah Griscom. Their son, in turn, married the assistant to steamboat pioneer John Fitch. The life of his sons, however, would not be as gentle. As part of fate's plan, upon Samuel's twenty-first birthday in 1730, he received full title for the property. He married Mary Livezey, and the couple had two daughters, Mary and Martha. The Pennsylvania yeoman lived happily at the property, attending the Quaker Meeting and maintaining the farm until Samuel's death in 1757. At the dawn of the French and Indian conflict, the problems of the growing city began to rub elbows with the peaceful aesthetic of the Bolton Farm.

Faced with the hardships of keeping her family together, Samuel's widow, Mary, soon married Joseph Paul and moved the family to Valley Forge. Coincidentally, the Pauls lived in the same house where George Washington would stay decades later during the Continental army's famous encampment there. The Paul family, who inherited the Bolton Farm by marriage, slowly began selling off the homestead's assets.

By 1773, the entire estate had been purchased by fellow yeoman Isaac Jones. The Jones family had been spreading out over much of eastern Montgomery County since their arrival almost a century before. Isaac's ownership of the property lasted only six years before he died in 1779. Before his death, however, Isaac willed the property to his seventy-nine-year-old brother, John, who already had a family of eleven children. John, in turn, deeded the Cheltenham estate to his youngest son, Amos, and died nine years later. His will reads in part:

> *I, John Jones of the township of Cheltenham…being weak of body through old age and infirmity yet of sound mind…give to my son Amos Jones all of my household goods, implements of husbandry as an addition to what I have heretofore given him.*

By the time of John's death in 1788, Amos had started a family of his own in the tiny, eighty-year-old fieldstone square. Amos, a gardener, married Ann Phipps of Philadelphia, and the couple had two children, Amos Jr. and Rebecca. In about 1790, at the peak of revolutionary fervor in Philadelphia, Amos gracefully avoided the chaos of the riled city and began building a large addition to his outdated home. Once completed, the Federal-style northeastern portion of the house dwarfed its older appendage. The typical Pennsylvania fieldstone farmhouse was fairly modest for the time—two and a half stories high, with a cellar.

In 1817, Amos Jr. acquired the property from his dying father and named the estate Pleasant Hill. Amos Jr. and his wife, Alice, were active Quakers at Abington Friends Meeting until Long Island Quaker Elias Hicks's controversial proposal that access to one's "inner light" need not depend on the Holy Bible caused the Hicksite/Orthodox split in 1827. Abington Meeting, like most in the area, was

Heidelberg's final section was this small guesthouse, which was added in about 1895. In this photo from 2010, its crumbling profile strangely resembles facial features.

torn in half by the schism. Although Hicks's "Hicksite" customs—which held a strong abolitionist presence—have become the standard for contemporary Quakerism, the new concept was not overwhelmingly popular at its inception. The split affected the Jones family rather personally. Amos Jr., who was a proponent of Hicks's philosophies, moved his family to the new Hicksite Meeting. But some of his family did not share his views and remained with the traditional Orthodox Meeting. This caused an apparent rift within the Jones family and sadly damaged their relations.

Amos Jr. sold Pleasant Hill to Robert Haines in 1850 and moved less than a mile away, where he died in 1865. Robert Haines, of the wealthy Germantown family, served on the Abington School Board and was later its president. He was also active in the Abington Hicksite Meeting, to which he contributed financially. When Haines and his fiancée, Margaret Wistar (also from an old monied Germantown family), were ready to tie the knot in 1850, the Jones property, consisting of one hundred acres, seemed like an idyllic new place to start a life. Before ever moving into the house, Robert had its largest section added. The three-story south wing, with its fish scale patterned Mansard roof and projecting gabled windows, was at the height of its style upon its completion in 1852, when Robert's marriage to Margaret took place.

After the wedding, the couple moved into their new dream home. The addition of the south wing brought the house to mansion status, and Robert completed the look with a flat-roof porch above the front entrance of the Federal-style northeast wing. The decoration of the mid-nineteenth-century addition clearly contrasted with the humble farmhouse from which it grew. Celebrating their common lineage—a frequent practice among rich families of the day—Robert and Margaret renamed the house Heidelberg, after the homeland of their families in Germany. The couple's love

for horticulture led to the establishment of the Cheltenham Nurseries on their vast property in 1857. It came to include many rare plants, including *Franklinia*, which was planted from a sapling taken from the Wistars' century-old garden at Wyck, their Germantown home. *Franklinia* was discovered by colonial botanist John Bartram in about 1760 and named for his friend Benjamin Franklin.

The couple had their first child, Caspar Wistar Haines, in 1853 and would eventually add five more to the count. The children all became prominent citizens in later years and would all remember Heidelberg fondly. Robert was loyal to his religious beliefs and never strayed from his duties at Abington Friends Meeting. He was also very philanthropic, building schools and donating to Quaker institutions when possible. The family also graciously hosted traveling missionaries at the house and accommodated those in need who were referred by the Society of Friends. Margaret made it a priority to make their experiences so delightful that they might consider joining the meeting. This is what led to her request by 1890 of another addition to the house, purely for the entertainment of guests.

Robert added the final limb of the house—the west wing—in 1891. It followed the same architectural scheme as the south wing, with a Mansard roof and gabled windows, but was a smaller two stories. The rather spacious apartment contained a kitchen and dining room on the first floor and three separate bedrooms on the second. The Haineses' home now held a distinction as one of the largest estates in Cheltenham, and the family was thriving. Robert's sudden death in 1895, however, threw a dark veil over Heidelberg. Margaret lived there with her daughters until 1912, when Caspar returned from Mexico, where he was employed in the railroad industry. Upon his aunt Jane Thompson's death, Caspar and his two surviving sisters—

This winter view from an upstairs bedroom in Heidelberg's southern block conjures up crackling fires, carriage rides in the snow and a strong sense of Victorian American life.

Reclaimed by nature, Heidelberg's original pre-colonial face is unwittingly highlighted in this 2011 photo. The house's original center block—built in about 1700—is sandwiched between a larger eighteenth-century addition to its left and an 1890s guesthouse wing to its right.

Mary and Jane—inherited her estate, which consisted of the Wistar family's centuries-old home, Wyck. While Mary and Jane chose to stay at Heidelberg, Caspar moved into Wyck, where he lived until his death. Margaret died in 1917 at an advanced age of eighty-seven, and the Heidelberg estate passed to the next closest son, Diedrick Jansen Haines.

It is not clear who lived at the property after Margaret's death, but upon the death of Diedrick in 1943, the house was sold along with the rest of the Haines estate. In 1944, a pair of couples moved into the house. Sisters Elizabeth and Jane (maiden name of Milnor), along with their husbands, John Bowker and Hugh McLaughlin, respectively, found their new home rich with history and, fortunately, appreciated it. The couples chose to rename the house again, in a quite personal way. The Bowkers and McLaughlins decided to call their home Kerlin Farm, a clever blending of the last three letters of the two last names. The two couples lived at the house, revamping and maintaining the Cheltenham Nurseries and keeping the historic spirit of the house alive.

Both couples had children before and after moving into Kerlin. As the 1950s plowed through the desirable suburb and new residential communities developed, the families sold off portions of the land to help keep up the old structure as costs rose. By the 1970s, the house had been passed down to Betty Barclay, daughter of Elizabeth and John Bowker, who did her best to maintain the house with her husband, James. Upon his departure from the home, Betty continued living at Kerlin with her three children. But by the 1980s, Betty had moved to a retirement community in Maryland, and her youngest son, Ian, maintained the house. While still in Betty's name, Ian lived alone at the estate, which had dwindled down to eight acres.

The historic home began its descent in the hands of Ian Barclay, who seemed to not even attempt maintenance on the house. While filing for historic landmark status, Ian was running a tax-free lumber business on the property, and his battles with the Township of Cheltenham would be frequent. While the task of solely maintaining a house of this size and age is certainly no easy one, the township claimed that Ian had not produced one example of a building improvement. After receiving local media attention in the late 1980s, it would seem that the house and surrounding property became something of an eyesore to the community. Ian himself became a rather notorious character as well in the eyes of local authorities.

In the 1990s, Reverend Ian Barclay, with his bushy beard and long ponytail, was in his forties and had become almost repulsive to the snippy surrounding neighborhood. He was eventually committed to Norristown State Hospital, and while the home was still owned by Betty—who was in no shape to care for it—Kerlin's state of abandonment began. It sat throughout the rest of the twentieth century with no inhabitants. Being located in a low-crime area, thankfully the house was spared vandalism and graffiti. Instead, the elements slowly worked on the house, giving it the prototypical haunted house look. In 2004, it was put on the endangered properties list, creating a spark of interest among historians. Sadly, the complicated battle between Betty Bowker, the township and an army of hungry real estate developers eventually claimed the house in 2012.

This particular piece of masonry and woodwork has proven historically unconventional in a variety of senses. One of its most interesting aspects was the natural sequence of its construction. It's an uncommon blend of architectural styles, from its tiny, pre-colonial origin and Federal-style enlargement to its Gilded Age, Second Empire–style southern and western additions—complete with Mansard roof—all wrapped up like a historical gift. Although the twentieth century played its role as the third complete century the home would see, it did not become significant to most living today until the twenty-first. Hopefully, it can be remembered and perhaps learned from, as one of the area's most personal examples of three hundred years of life in Pennsylvania.

CHAPTER 7

MEMORIAM

Like any other city with a large population, Philadelphia contains a vast number of cemeteries and burial grounds. In the years of Pennsylvania as a colony, most families chose to inter their loved ones at their local church cemeteries or on their estates themselves. Since the city had no shortage of churches, meetinghouses and places of worship, many residents were buried in the small churchyards that surrounded them. Most of these tiny burial grounds have vanished from the landscape, but some still exist. Some churchyards of the older congregations filled up before 1730, and additional land purchases were needed. Christ Church, founded in 1695, is surrounded by a pre-revolutionary burial ground. But by 1716, the widening city had surrounded Christ Church. New land for a burial ground was purchased in 1719 four blocks away at Fifth and Arch Streets, then the "outskirts of town," as anything farther west was forest. There the Christ Church Burial Ground still sits, behind a stone wall. It contains many important American founders, such as Benjamin Franklin, Benjamin Rush and Commodore William Bainbridge.

A few decades into the nineteenth century, it was very clear that crowded churchyards were unhealthy and impractical. Thoughts and feelings regarding the proper dispensation of the dead began changing. Once thought of as more of a ritualistic event, visitation of graves of loved ones became less somber and formal. The concept of erecting large physical monuments to commemorate one's life became more commercial and sociological. Following in the footsteps of Boston's Mount Auburn Cemetery, the nondenominational "park cemetery" was introduced in Philadelphia in 1836 with the opening of the Laurel Hill Cemetery. A new concept, the park cemetery acted as a place of public leisure and refuge. The idea of decorating the place where the dead rest was a shaky new idea at the time. However, it was also a marketable idea. In the 1850s, several other park cemetery companies purchased land around the city. Thinking ahead, most purchased tracts of remote land, far detached from any populated areas. By the close of the Civil War, park cemeteries had fast become accepted—due to the urgent need of burial space if nothing else.

As the Industrial Revolution proceeded and the Civil War ended, Philadelphia's park cemeteries became an industry of their own, competing with one another through advertising and political and legal back-and-forths. The time from the post–Civil War period until the end of the century was probably the best in America for park cemeteries. Under Victorian-era beliefs and customs, these cities of the dead thrived. Their heavenly display of love for the bygone souls they represented was the ultimate example of affection. The twentieth century would slowly change this attitude, however, and the cemetery business would begin to lose its appeal to investors. As Philadelphia modernized itself by necessity, through depression and war, its fantastical relationship with its dead would also mature.

By the twenty-first century, the concept of extravagant burial monuments had become a historic institution in itself. Most park cemeteries operate today using state or city funds, as well as occasional plot sales. The Philadelphia area contains many scenic park cemeteries, some of which are listed on the National Register of Historic Places. However, a number of them have simply not survived in business form and have since fallen into a state of neglect and abandonment. This chapter will clear away the brush from two such burial grounds and delve into their compelling pasts.

Mount Vernon Cemetery

IN 1856, TWO YEARS AFTER Philadelphia's consolidation, the Mount Vernon Cemetery Company was founded. In an attempt to capitalize on the seemingly charmed success of Laurel Hill Cemetery, the trustees of Mount Vernon Cemetery Company purchased land directly across Ridge Avenue from Laurel Hill. The land had been part of Mount Peace, the colonial estate of the Ralston family. Robert Ralston, founder of the Church of Saint James the Less in 1846, lived there at the time. The cemetery company's first treasurer, Robert Buist, worked closely with his friends and owners of Laurel Hill, purchasing additional acreage from the adjacent cemetery. The cemetery's nearly seventy-five acres bordered Lehigh Avenue (then Hart Lane) to the south, Ridge Avenue and Hunting Park Avenue (then Nicetown Lane) to the west and the rest of the Ralston property to the north and east. The remaining Ralston land would later be purchased by the Odd Fellows for their new park cemetery, which carried on the name of the former Ralston estate, Mount Peace.

Not surprisingly, the architect of Laurel Hill's landscape as well as its Italianate gatehouse, John Notman, was called on to design a bigger, better gatehouse for Mount Vernon. Notman and Buist had been longtime friends and had arrived in America together on the *Thames*. After some discussion over the erection of the gatehouse, it was decided that "the Committee on Improvements be authorized to contract for the building of the tower. Two sides of marble and two sides of cut square stone and the remainder as proposed, provided the amount does not exceed thirty-four hundred dollars and occasion delay of more than one month."

Attached to the gatehouse was a living quarters for the groundskeeper. However, dissatisfaction over the delay of its construction caused some friction. Meanwhile, the layout of Mount Vernon's grounds was arranged by G.M. Hopkins Jr. Its grand circle and rolling hillside were not uncommon of cemeteries of the time. Many of Mount Vernon's first interments lay just beyond its gatehouse, where their tall marble columns and obelisks seem to thrust skyward. Many are topped with statues of angels whose right arms are extended above their heads, pointing up toward the heavenly destination of the souls they represent.

In September 1857, Mount Vernon superintendent William Linten wrote monthly to Buist, informing him of the progress of construction: "The dwelling house has been roofed and the floors laid. The marble and stonework on the tower is all done...The circles are ready for marble work."

In August, Linten wrote, "The work on the tower is well on towards completion...The marble work on the entrance goes on slowly. The two small side arches, over the footways are finished, the arch over the carriageway spring, and two of the figures ready to be put up."

When the gatehouse was finally completed in 1858, its landmark bell tower could be seen for blocks, and the clean-cut Italian marble of its façade stood tall over its neighbor, Laurel Hill. Notman was paid a total of $400 for his work, and according to Buist in 1859, the cost of the entire project—including paving, curbing, installation of gutters, landscaping and the erection of the gatehouse—was $35,330. In the book *John Notman: Architect*, author Constance Greiff described the completed gatehouse

Mount Vernon Cemetery's army of stone angels often points toward the heavens. Today, their cold fingers act as perches for hawks, eagles and other rare birds. The rustic property's ironic location in the urban jungle of North Philadelphia is one of its more compelling contrasts.

as "the setting for an Italian fairytale," with an "ethereal and dream-like quality." Today, the gatehouse is missing its signature tower, which collapsed. Covered in rampant overgrowth, its majesty is no longer gleaming. Notman died at age fifty-five in 1865 and was interred across the street at Laurel Hill. By then, it was clear that park cemeteries existed more to pacify the living than to serve the dead.

Although quickly filling up with ornate sculptures and stones, Mount Vernon received its most coveted monument in 1864: the Gardel monument. The fact that little is known about the Gardel family adds more mystery to the monument's ominous presence. Julia Hawkes Gardel was a Philadelphia schoolteacher, founder of a women's seminary school and an advocate for better public schools. She married fellow teacher and art collector Bertrand Gardel, who was absurdly well off for a French language teacher. His art collection was sought after upon his death, and his ability to tour the globe with his wife, purchasing art and jewelry, clearly demonstrated his status of wealth. He was a friend of famed artist Thomas Eakins and even appears in one of Eakins's paintings. According to a *Philadelphia Inquirer* article of 1871, Mrs. Gardel was on a "world tour," traveling from Jerusalem to Damascus, when she was "attacked by the Bedouins" and killed. Clearly a shocking end for an apparently endearing woman, her husband responded to his grief financially.

While an obvious show of fortune, the incredible monument erected to Julia Gardel by her devastated husband in 1864 is also the most unique and personalized expression of Victorian romantic tragedy that exists in any cemetery in Philadelphia. The twenty-five-foot monument, made from Ohio sandstone, Italian marble and imported granite, cost an unbelievable $36,000—the equivalent of about $2 million today. Designed by famed Belgian

sculptor G. Geef, the giant pyramid was fronted by a host of statuary displaying Julia's love of traveling the world. Large marble figures represent the continents of Asia, Europe and Africa. Perched above the pyramid door are statues of Hope and Faith holding up a carved relief of Julia. Mount Vernon's trustees used drawings and photographs of the monument in their sales brochures, and it soon became the cemetery's mascot. Bertrand finally followed his wife into the vault in 1895.

In 1867, the cemetery acquired more than 2,500 graves from the crowded Second Presbyterian Church burial ground on Arch Street, most of which dated from the early eighteenth century. Included were several Revolutionary War heroes like George Washington's secretary of war Henry Knox, as well as noted historical characters like author Peter Stephen DuPonceau and Reverend Peletiah Webster (the "Forgotten Founding Father"). Although not known to most and largely ignored by history, Webster was hailed as one of the most important figures in the creation of the United States Constitution. The old churchyard plot also contains the remains of Constitutional Congressman William Houston. Sadly, theirs are some of the many original unreadable stones from the Second Presbyterian churchyard, and their exact locations cannot be determined. Cemetery company treasurer Robert Buist himself became a resident at Mount Vernon upon his death in 1880. Over the years, Mount Vernon received other notable interments, such as brewery owner Louis Bergdoll Jr. and actress Dorothy McHugh, who's single line on a TV commercial became legendary: "I've fallen and I can't get up!" Actress Judy Lewis, an illegitimate child of Clark Gable and Loretta Young, best known for her role on *General Hospital*, also rests at Mount Vernon. But perhaps its most famous interments are the Drew family.

Louisa Lane Drew was an aspiring actress at the Arch Street Theater in the 1850s and '60s. She later married

These two-hundred-year-old gravestones from the Second Presbyterian Church Burial Ground in Old City—moved to Mount Vernon Cemetery in 1867—have been mercilessly battered by the elements. Sadly, the original colonial markers are indecipherable.

the owner of the theater, John Drew. Upon his death in 1862, Louisa became the theater's new owner and operated it herself with success. Louisa became the grandmother of Hollywood superstars John, Lionel and Ethel Barrymore. She died in 1897 and was buried with her late husband at Mount Vernon. The Drews' small plot received its last interment in 1980. John Barrymore, best known for his roles in *Richard III* and *Hamlet*, died in Hollywood in 1942. Although his will stated that he wished to be buried in the Drew lot at Mount Vernon, his body was interred at Cavalry Cemetery in Los Angeles. His funeral was attended by some of the most prolific actors of the century.

After decades of rest, however, John Barrymore's body was removed by his son, John Barrymore Jr. (father of actress Drew Barrymore). In December 1980, John Jr., in his truly odd fashion, had the remains of his father removed and cremated. It is said that John Jr. couldn't resist the opportunity to take a peak at his father's body before it was cremated. He then personally flew the ashes to Philadelphia. Showing up in the middle of the night, stoned, with his father's ashes in a suitcase, John Jr. eventually followed the proper channels and left instruction on where to bury the little bag containing the remains of the most legendary actor of the day.

Finally, on December 12, 1980, Barrymore's remains were reburied in the Drew plot at Mount Vernon. No one was present at John Barrymore's long awaited reunion with his parents except the undertaker and John Jr., who reportedly stated, "Now it is finished." Leaving as fast as he came, John Jr. flew back to Los Angeles the next day and apparently never

returned to his father's final resting place. No stone or marker of any kind was purchased. In fact, the presence of Barrymore's grave was largely unknown until 1997, when a group of fans and donors erected a small stone on which is engraved one of his best-known lines: "Alas poor Yorick." Even today, most people are not aware that John Barrymore rests in Philadelphia. Hopefully in the future, with some encouragement (and landscaping), the Drew plot can host new surprised visitors and old devoted fans.

Today, Mount Vernon Cemetery is like a wildlife refuge in the middle of the inner city. Nature has reclaimed most of the grounds, hiding its beauty with weeds and brush. The cemetery is not open to the public, and with an out-of-state owner and only occasional visits by volunteer groundskeepers, its historic monuments are held captive from would-be visitors. Some of the mausoleums have been vandalized, and others are in danger. A fence secures the property, but the centuries-old oak trees whose branches wither and collapse and the wild vines that wrap and twist around the fragile monuments are the real dangers to this once proud safe keeper of Philadelphia's past.

Mount Vernon, however, remains one of Philadelphia's most interesting yet underappreciated pieces of land. Given its former social status, its notable interments, its collection of unique monuments, its history and its location, the cemetery's presence is intriguing enough. But top it off with overgrowth, neglect and decay, and what emerges is an almost fantastical, irrational environment. Its cloudy geography and mysterious appearance offer up curious historical perspectives nearly too enticing for urban explorers to resist.

The twenty-foot pyramid erected for Julia Gardel represents Victorian romantic tragedy like no other monument in Philadelphia. Her bereaved husband paid more than $30,000 for its construction in 1864, the equivalent of about $2 million today.

OPPOSITE One of Mount Vernon's more elaborate stones, the Keller monument features a ten-foot-tall cross and base—carved from a single piece of stone—and a life-size statue.

ABOVE This modest stone is better than none at all for Hollywood legend John Barrymore. It was purchased and placed atop his unmarked grave at Mount Vernon Cemetery in 1997 by a devoted group of fans.

It is a virtual puzzle, featuring real historical characters and parameters, that offers real rewards of knowledge and comprehension to anyone willing to solve its thousands of challenges. The majesty of Mount Vernon Cemetery definitely makes it a site worth saving.

The rear of Stephen Button's 1855 Norman gatehouse at Mount Moriah Cemetery gathers trash in 2008. It once housed the cemetery's offices and groundskeeper's quarters.

Mount Moriah Cemetery

THE CONCEPT OF BURYING our dead is as old as humanity itself. The concept of *marking* the ground where the dead lay is not much younger. But the idea of building a grand, permanent monument to oneself—meant literally to last forever—was an act reserved only for kings until the last millennia. With the success of Laurel Hill, Philadelphia's first park cemetery, several profit-hungry groups of investors and businessmen began buying land to lay out other park cemeteries. By the 1850s, the cemetery business had become a profitable one, as several new park cemeteries emerged in Philadelphia, including Mount Vernon, Cedar Hill, Mount Lawn, William Penn, the Woodlands and others. On March 27, 1855, the Mount Moriah Cemetery Company—whose board was largely made up of local Freemasons—was granted a permit for fifty-four acres fronting Philadelphia's southwestern border, Cobb's Creek.

Stretching from a point near the current intersection of Cemetery and Kingsessing Avenues west to the creek, the original portion of the property was chosen due to its position at the top of a sloping hill, then the highest elevation in the area. Before row homes, telephone poles and streetlamps, the view from the peak of the hill would have been breathtaking. The layout of the original portion cleverly utilized the sweeping landscape in the plan of its roadways, with its two main circles crowning the summits of its two highest peaks. By October 1855, the first circle was completed, followed by its diametrically crossed footpaths. Its grand entrance gatehouse would be fronting the circle on the property's eastern edge.

In the park cemetery business of the mid-nineteenth century, the gatehouse was a cemetery's most important showpiece, acting as its visual slogan. Therefore, Mount Moriah's Masonic board of trustees took its time deciding on the perfect face for its dreamy, pseudo-spiritual park of memories. From a host of other submitted designs, architect Stephen Decatur Button's plan for a brownstone Norman gatehouse was the chosen entry. His experience as a noted church architect shows in the simple placement of the gatehouse. But the subtle Masonic influence is also present in the way in which it was built to face the rising of the sun. It featured a single gated arch that Button capped with an imposing statue of Father Time, who gazed down on visitors as they entered, like a morbid reminder.

Although spirituality played a significant role in the Mount Moriah Cemetery Company's actions, it was, after all, a business, and selling plots was the main objective. The ways that several of the city's park cemeteries were able to achieve success in the days before the Civil War is interesting. For instance, a few succeeded in purchasing the remains of famous historical individuals and bygone revolutionary heroes for reinterment. In 1857, after some political and financial negotiations, the remains of Elizabeth Griscom Ross Claypoole (Betsy Ross) were removed from the Free Quaker Burial Ground at Fifth and Arch Streets and reinterred at Mount Moriah along with her sisters and her husband, John Claypoole. Fraternal and charity-based organizations would raise money year after year for the upkeep and beautification of Ross's grave. The Daughters of the American Revolution erected a flagpole there and kept a flag raised atop it for decades. Only the flagpole remains today.

When the Reading Railroad laid its tracks along the main line in the late 1850s, it connected the city to the new cemetery. Mount Moriah Station was opened at Kingsessing and Cemetery Avenues soon after, and the sale of plots quickly rose. Shortly after the close of the Civil War, the cemetery encompassed almost two hundred acres, stretching equally on both sides of Philadelphia's western border with Yeadon, Delaware County. A large plot for soldiers was purchased on the Philadelphia side of the property. It was paid for by many of the same philanthropists who ran the Volunteer Refreshment Saloons, which operated throughout the city during the war. The soldiers' plot was full by 1866 and contained Confederate as well as Union soldiers, a rare practice in the area. Other military plots were soon purchased, such as the Philadelphia Soldier's Home plot and the Naval Hospital plot.

Fraternal organizations, needless to say, were the largest purchasers of plot space at Mount Moriah. Lots belonging to local Masonic, Odd Fellows and Elks Lodges patch the landscape of the cemetery. The property's expansive acreage was perfect for the construction of common vaults for large occupancies such as these. The cemetery company's president, John H. Jones, attempted to further mystify Mount Moriah's image by giving the roads, circles and even Cobb's Creek new names. The Circle of Saint John, the second circle, was laid out in 1856 for the Keystone Chapter of Pennsylvania's Grand Lodge. The Glen of Silence was the name of the area along the Cobb's Creek, on the Philadelphia side, now occupied by the Cobb's Creek Parkway. Some early maps even refer to the creek as the Stream of Kedron.

Local private institutions like the Presbyterian Home for Widows and Single Women and the Seaman's Church Institute were the second-biggest purchasers of large plots. The small community of Kingsessing was expanding away from the cemetery,

Until recently, vines and weeds had imprisoned much of Mount Moriah's eloquent Victorian statuary. The Friends of Mount Moriah Cemetery, a nonprofit volunteer group, is working to free the monuments from their natural bondage.

and the railroad also brought new development to the area. Seeing this as a hindrance to its idyllic atmosphere of shady trees and babbling brooks, the cemetery's board quickly bought up more surrounding land. By 1870, the property contained more acreage on both the Philadelphia and Yeadon sides. But the cemetery truly came into its own in 1871, when the Circle of Saint John received its centerpiece: the Schnider monument.

When Grand Tyler William Bockius Schnider died in 1867, the members of his chapter had him placed in a vault in the now-defunct Monument Cemetery until their momentous plans for his funerary procedure could be solidified. Having served as "Grand Tyler" for more than two decades at Samuel Sloan's Gothic Masonic Temple on Broad Street—before it was destroyed by fire in 1886—Schnider proved a beloved brother to his fellow Masons. In 1871, the members erected a thirty-five-foot-tall monument for him—the largest and tallest in the city at the time. The giant Ionic column was made of imported Italian marble and capped with a Masonic square and compass. The triangular marble base of the monument featured a carved bust of Schnider on one side, Masonic symbols on another and the altar and Bible on the third. The total cost of the monument was $7,500, equivalent to about $200,000 today. In 1874, the death of cemetery company president John H. Jones affected Mount Moriah forever. Per Jones's request, upon his burial, the statue of Father Time that sat on top of the gatehouse was removed and placed atop his large stone, which sits just behind the gatehouse.

As in most cemeteries of the period, the more expensive plots featured large monuments and underground vaults. These plots were usually situated in the circles and along the main roads, while the less expensive majority of burials filled in the midsections. The not-uncommon custom of the day at park cemeteries like Mount Moriah of planting exotic imported trees and flowers at the graves of loved ones gave the cemetery another unique role as host to some rare flora. Well-groomed bushes and saplings, decorated by a frontage of colorful flowers and a backdrop of weeping trees, transformed the artistic statuary of the stones and monuments into a visual Eden. Some types of decorative trees caught on almost immediately as a trend in many cemeteries, such as the odd-looking Japanese pines that grew in the shape of mushroom clouds. Others became less desirable due to cost or availability. But today, Mount Moriah is ironically one of the few places in the Delaware Valley to view some of these exotic trees.

By 1890, Mount Moriah housed more notable interments, such as world-famous stage actor John McCullough. Born in Ireland in 1832, McCullough's career was one of the most impressive of any Victorian-era Philadelphia actor. He arrived in Philadelphia in 1847, having fled the famine of Ireland at his father's insistence. Under the management of John Drew, McCullough played his first acting role—that of Thomas in *The Bell's Stratagem*—at Drew's Arch Street Theater in 1857. Like many actors of the time, it was McCullough's nagging persistence that furthered his career. Stage roles, especially for Irish immigrants, were very hard to come by in the mid-nineteenth century. McCullough mingled with other actors and theater folk of the day, such as Edwin Booth (father of John Wilkes), Edwin Forrest and Frederick Warde.

Under the management of D.C. theater owner John T. Ford, McCullough played his favorite role (the one that would also be his most famous), "Virginius" in *Hamlet*. By 1884, McCullough was showing signs of "feeble-mindedness" and retired from the stage. He was committed to the Bloomingdale Sanitarium in New York before returning to his home in Philadelphia, where he died in 1885. When McCullough

The monument of former Mount Moriah Cemetery Company president John H. Jones supports a solemn statue of Father Time, which once sat atop the gatehouse glaring at entering visitors.

was buried in 1887, his funeral was said to be one of the largest in Philadelphia memory. His monument was said to be, at the time, the tallest ever erected for an actor. It featured a life-size bronze bust of McCullough that, sadly, has since been stolen. The arrangement of his monument and the choreography of his funeral procession took more than a year of preparation, and it was attended by more than five hundred guests.

The 1890s, probably the last great decade for Gilded Age money, were transitional years at Mount Moriah. New city charter laws and regulations, increased taxes and the first subtle hints of the slow decline of the park cemetery in America rained dark forebodings on the future of the cemetery. The turn of the twentieth century brought a slight decrease in the frequency of expensive, towering monuments, a trend that would continue into the 1930s. The First World War brought more public attention to the city's cemeteries, and a trend of war monuments swept Philadelphia. Many old monuments were restored, and a sense of appreciation for history seemed to drive Philadelphians. The 1920s were no less sparing. The rising economy seemed to briefly boost the sale of plots at Mount Moriah, but by 1928, the cemetery had begun cutting back on its printed ads. The property expanded again in the 1930s, when the adjacent Fels and Paschall properties on the Philadelphia side were purchased, bringing the property to its current four hundred acres or thereabouts.

Depression-era work programs like the Works Progress Administration also enhanced the grounds at Mount Moriah by improving its aged and failing drainage system, connecting it to a culverted stream that formerly cut through the property. The Second World War brought a new wave of internments to Mount Moriah, overfilling the soldiers' plot. The surrounding neighborhood began its ethnic changes in the late 1950s, and the cemetery business in Philadelphia was not what it once was. The last financial decline for Mount Moriah began slowly in the 1960s. Many of the big plot holders, such as the Keystone Lodge and the Benevolent and Protective Order of Elks Lodge, had filled up their century-old plots decades before. Most had either relocated or closed their local institutions by 1970, and those resting beneath the Circle of Saint John became only distant, unknown relatives. The once prestigious Keystone Chapter's circle was quickly forgotten and began growing into the jungle it is today.

One of the more interesting events in the cemetery's history took place in 1975, when city officials—in preparation for the bicentennial celebration—removed the remains of Betsy Ross from her overgrown prison at Mount Moriah. They were reinterred in the side court of the newly renovated Betsy Ross House on Arch Street, in the hopes of attracting more visitors to the economically dry city. However, the Claypoole plot at Mount Moriah was in a sad state of ruin by the 1970s. Ross's headstone had been stolen years before, and the others were covered in weeds and debris and were unreadable. Although *someone* was removed from the plot, it was never *exactly* clear whom. In the years following, and still today, the question of who was actually removed and reburied is an interesting topic among local historians. The remains of America's most beloved seamstress may still lie beneath the weeds in Southwest Philadelphia.

One of Mount Moriah's more recent famous interments was that of legendary Motown producer John Whitehead, pioneer of "that Philly sound," who died in 2004. Evidence suggests, however, that his remains have since been relocated. Later that year, the still operating Mount Moriah Cemetery Association's last living member, Horatio Jones Jr., died, throwing the property's legal administration into a state of life support. Held together by the efforts of a loyal employee of the association, the cemetery legally remained in business, although burials were scarce. Its last were those of Muslims, who predominated the neighborhood of Kingsessing by the turn of the twenty-first century. Mount Moriah was, at the time, the only nondenominational cemetery in Philadelphia that allowed Muslim burials.

As attention to the grounds dropped off the city's priority list, it went into a sort of coma, remaining in limbo and becoming a common dumping ground. Kept shielded from curious visitors by the neighborhood's negative reputation, the long-overgrown Circle of Saint John section grew into a small forest, as did the original circle behind the historic gatehouse. By 2008, the rustic cemetery—hiding burned-out cars, illegal dogfighting arenas and, in some cases, nonresident corpses—had become enough of a problem to begin appearing in the local and national news. But with no official owner on which to place legal and financial blame, Mount Moriah had become a real thorn in the city's side, and officials fought to avoid inheriting the property. Police found the miles of broken cemetery roadway—which was often blocked up by piles of trash—too difficult or impossible to regularly patrol. Its vast acreage of weeds, trees and winding roads resembled a nature park, complete with wildlife.

In 2011, according to city reports, the Mount Moriah Cemetery Association ceased its business interests without informing the City of Philadelphia or the Borough of Yeadon. The illegal act sparked the beginning of another court battle, which further held up any actual property maintenance. However, the nonprofit organization Friends of Mount Moriah Cemetery—a group of devoted historians and local residents—was thankfully able to gain temporary legal ownership of the property. Since 2011, mostly through volunteer efforts, the group has cleared roads, removed overgrowth and removed every old car on the property. Today, Friends of Mount Moriah continues its hard work to keep the property clean and safe for other curious visitors.

The thirty-five-foot monument to William B. Schnider, Grand Tyler of Pennsylvania's Central Grand Lodge, marks the center of the overgrown Circle of Saint John at Mount Moriah, a popular burial site of nineteenth-century Freemasons.

BIBLIOGRAPHY

Evening Bulletin articles. Property of Temple University, Special Collections Research Center.

Evening Public Ledger articles. Property of the Library of Congress, Chronicling America: Historic American Newspapers site, found at http://chroniclingamerica.loc.gov.

Philadelphia Inquirer articles. Property of the *Philadelphia Inquirer*.

Chapter 1

Evening Bulletin. "Liversidge Made Director." February 25, 1936.

Patten, W.N. "Construction Features of Delaware Waterside Power Station of the Philadelphia Electric Company." *Stone and Webster Journal*, 1922.

Wainwright, Nicholas B. *History of the Philadelphia Electric Company, 1881–1961.* Philadelphia, PA: Philadelphia Electric Company, 1961.

Chapter 2

Automobile Topics Magazine 28 (1912): 1,003.

Evening Public Ledger. "Secret Formula Bread Scouted." October 6, 1917.

Hudson, Sam. *Pennsylvania and Its Public Men.* Philadelphia, PA: Hudson and Joseph, 1909.

Moody's Magazine 17 (January 1914): 102.

Philadelphia War History Committee. *Philadelphia in the World War, 1914–1919.* New York: Wynkoop-Hallenbeck-Crawford Publishing Company, 1922.

Philips, Camillus. *How They Did It.* New York: McGraw-Hill Publishing Company, 1920.

Scranton, Philip, and Walter Licht. *Work Sights: Industrial Philadelphia, 1890–1950.* Philadelphia, PA: Temple University Press, 1986.

Spaulding, Harold E. *Workshop of the World.* N.p.: Oliver Evans Press, 1990. Accessed at www.workshopoftheworld.com.

Tasty Baking Company. *Tastykake: 50 Years of Quality, 1914–1964.* Property of Temple University Special Collections Research Center, Philadelphia, Pennsylvania.

Chapter 3

Clark, Robert Wayne. *The Thomas A. Edison High School: A Report to Our Community.* Philadelphia, PA: Northeast High School, 1957.

Michener, A.O. *A History of the Northeast High School, Philadelphia.* Philadelphia, PA: John C. Winston Company, 1938.

Chapter 4

Historical Society of Pennsylvania. "Closed for Business: The Story of Bankers Trust Company During the Great Depression." http://www.hsp.org/bankers-trust.

Pittsburg Dispatch. August 4, 1891.

Reynoldsville [PA] *Star.* November 9, 1898, 3.

Shenndoah [PA] *Evening Herald.* June 9, 1891, 3.

Slobodzian, Joseph A. "Building Owner Admits Faulty Asbestos Work, an Inexperienced Crew Left a Dangerous Mess in a North Philadelphia Tower." *Philadelphia Inquirer*, July 18, 1995.

Chapter 5

Ahern, Joseph-James. *Philadelphia Naval Shipyard.* Charleston, SC: Arcadia Publishing, 1997.

Clement, Dan. *Written Historical and Descriptive Data—Frankford Arsenal, Bridge and Tacony Streets, Philadelphia, Pennsylvania.* Historic American Engineering Record (HAER) PA-74, National Park Service, Department of the Interior, Washington D.C., 1984.

DeWolf, Rose. "Frankford Arsenal Museum in the Works." *Philadelphia Daily News*, September 19, 1991.

Dorwart, Jeffrey M., and Jean K. Wolf. *The Philadelphia Navy Yard.* Philadelphia: University of Pennsylvania Press, Barra Foundation, 2001.

Farley, James J. *Making Arms in the Machine Age: Philadelphia's Frankford Arsenal, 1816–1870.* University Park, PA: Penn State University Press, 1994.

Chapter 6

Gartner, Ellen. "History." Heidelberg Kerlin Farm. heidelbergkerlinfarm.wordpress.com/history.

Henry P. McIlhenny Papers. Articles, interviews and lectures series, Philadelphia Museum of Art Archives, Philadelphia, Pennsylvania.

Myers, Albert Cook. *Quaker Arrivals at Philadelphia.* Philadelphia, PA: Ferris and Leach, 1902.

Russell, John. "Henry P. McIlhenny." Obituary. *New York Times*, May 13, 1986.

Chapter 7

Friends of Mount Moriah Cemetery. friendsofmountmoriahcemetery.org.

Greiff, Constance M. *John Notman, Architect.* Philadelphia, PA: Athenaeum of Philadelphia, 1979.

Keels, Thomas H. *Wicked Philadelphia.* Charleston, SC: The History Press, 2010.

Winter, William. *In Memory of John McCullough.* New York: De Vinne Press, 1889.

INDEX

ABOUT THE AUTHOR

John Webster comes from a long line of Philadelphia families. His adventures have earned him the labels "guerrilla historian" and "urban explorer." John and his associates have investigated many of the Philadelphia area's abandoned historical structures. Webster has been featured in several newspaper and online articles and is regarded as one of Philadelphia's pioneers of urban exploration. He has taken hundreds of thousands of photos of his beloved city. His first book, *The Philadelphia State Hospital at Byberry: A History of Misery and Medicine*, was published in 2013. This is his second work.

Visit us at
www.historypress.net
....
This title is also available as an e-book.